The Secret to Your FUTURE HISTORY

Dream Realisation Technique

Dr Alan B Jones PhD

The Secret to Your FUTURE HISTORY

Dream Realisation Technique

OVERVIEW

This Book Is For You, About You and Your Future!

"Life is too short to waste any amount of time on wondering what other people think about you. In the first place, if they had better things going on in their lives, they wouldn't have the time to sit around and talk about you.

What's important to me is not others' opinions of me, but what's important to me is my opinion of myself."

C. JoyBell C.

Prologue

Several years ago, I was involved in a series of seminars on the subject of success.

One of the guest speakers was a man who had what would best be described as a rags-to-riches-to-rags story. He considered himself as a bit of a 'wheeler dealer' and through some interesting twists and turns of what he called 'fate' had won over a million pounds in a television game show.

By his own admission, he thought this to be the happiest time of his life. He lived the life of a 'winner'; he held amazing parties, bought properties, travelled. From the outside, it seemed as if this man had everything he could ever want.

Eighteen months after winning this amazing amount of money he was forced to go bankrupt. His life style had outstripped his dwindling means and a series of poor investments took their toll.

He realised that many of his so called 'friends' were of the 'good time' variety and the beautiful women who kept his company seemed to vanish as rapidly as his financial security.

It was a heartfelt and sobering presentation accompanied with pictures, newspaper stories and scrapbooks attesting to his now lost fortune and luck.

Fate, it seemed, had been a rather harsh mistress. As he concluded his talk he made to me what was a very profound statement. He said, 'you don't know what happiness is until the things that you believe make you happy have gone!'

Note, he said 'the things that **you believe** make you happy'...

This simple statement set me to thinking about the nature of happiness, and by extension the definition of success.

For the last twenty years I have been working with individuals, schools, colleges and major businesses exploring the how and what of motivation, achievement and change. At the core of all of this work has been the lingering question as to just what it is that makes us - you, me - happy.

I will share some of my thoughts in this book.

Future History

Before we go any further perhaps we need to explore what is meant by *Future History*.

I'm not an overly sporty or sports-loving person, but I do see within this realm of human endeavour examples of achievement and success. One of my sporting heroes is Muhammed Ali. Now for someone who does not like violence in any form, it may seem odd that I have chosen a boxer as a sporting icon.

Born Cassius Marcellus Clay Jnr in 1942, Ali became not only one of the greatest sporting legends of all time, but through is involvement with Malcolm X, an activist, supporter of racial integration and a campaigner for equality. A controversial man, to say the least, and one who was able to polarise public opinion hence provoking debate and discussion.

As an amateur boxer, his sporting record was pretty amazing - one hundred 'wins' and five 'losses'. The 'wins' included his Olympic Gold at the 1960 Olympics in Rome.

Upon turning professional he quickly created a record of 19 fights, with 19 'wins' with 15 of those through a 'knock-out'. He defeated 'Sonny Boy Liston' to become the Heavyweight Champion of the World in 1964 when he was 22 years old.

Throughout his career in the ring three things became immediately apparent to anyone who cared to watch.

For a heavy-weight this man could move - he developed the rhyme 'floats like a butterfly, stings like a bee' to remind everyone of this simple fact.

He had probably the best personal mission statement ever - "I am the greatest!", a phrase that could be seen as being a boastful conceit, but was one that was actually backed by an incredible work ethic.

Finally, and for our purposes the most relevant, he somehow seemed to predict his fights in advance. He would rhyme and state his intention that his opponent would 'go down' in round three, or four.

There was a run of seven times out of eight where he got it right – and when, in February 1962, he stopped Don Warner in four rather than the five he forecast, Ali claimed he had finished the fight early because Warner had not shaken hands.

This was not just great PR, but was based on techniques Muhammed Ali used in his training. When asked by a journalist how he could make these predictions, Ali apparently replied *It's because I have a FUTURE HISTORY'*. He had seen the fight in his head; during his training; in his preparation and whilst standing waiting to go into the ring. He was using a visualisation technique supported by focussed work and detailed preparation.

We will explore this kind of technique in this book allowing you to create your own Future History.

I am an ordinary man who worked hard to develop the talent I was given. I believed in myself, and I believe in the goodness of others.

Muhammed Ali

Why This Book?

Is this a Self-Help book?

Yes, in many ways this is a self-help, personal development kind-of-a-book, and I certainly hope it will help you reflect on key aspects of your life. However, there is a real problem with so many self-help books. Psychologists have noted that some styles of self-help books contain little in the way of help and can actually cause more harm than good.

Some of these kinds of books can reinforce perceptions of inferiority by using exceptional role models or presenting unrealistic rewards to those who follow the authors guidance. More relevantly there are self-help/personal development books 'out there' which state explicitly that if you do not get the rewards promised by the author and their book then it's *your fault* as you did not work hard enough or believe sufficiently in the beneficent powers of the Universe.

Many people who read self-help books are searching for some answers or ways to become 'unstuck' in their lives. When one author does not provide the immediate solution, then it's easy to go and find a new book, with a glossier cover - a new guru with a different spin on the same rhetoric. In this way self-help books can be seen as being another form of avoidance. By following the latest thirteen step pathway to a miracle cure, such books allow the reader to avoid key issues which may be at the core of their problems.

In a number of cases the methods suggested by the author in this kind of book lack any real psychological validation. They may present techniques that have been of value to the author, but to assume that they will have the same impact on others is questionable to say the least. The truth is that **no one else has your unique set of experiences, personal resources, talents, potentials or support networks.**

There is often a huge difference between these kinds of books written by those who have formally studied and trained within the fields of psychology, coaching and counselling and those written by well-meaning survivors of their own stories. Moreover, there are a number of books that appear to have a spiritual basis which suggest that once the affirmation or wish has been given over to the Cosmos, and providing you dedicate your-self to the belief, all will be as you dream. YOU have to do nothing else!

"A planner may find that their beautiful plans fail because they do not follow through with them. Like so many people they may believe that ideas move mountains. But, it is bulldozers that move mountains, it is the ideas which show them where to go."

Peter F Drucker

I am reminded of a client I worked with whose mother had committed suicide. My clients mother was a staunch Church goer, she had been diagnosed with bi-polar disorder. She was told by members of her congregation that if she prayed to God, her condition would go away, that she would no longer need to take tablets.

My clients mother prayed and prayed and for a short while the symptoms of her illness 'went away'.

Hallelujah!

However, soon her symptoms returned, as we might expect with her particular condition, and rather than being supportive those same members of her congregation suggested that this was because she had not prayed hard enough, or trusted in God enough. This criticism was all that was required to prompt this, unfortunate ladies suicide.

I had been asked to support the family through this, and understandably they themselves began to question the nature of their faith and belief in a just and loving God.

This is perhaps one of my motivations for wanting to write this book. I want to offer some tools which are based upon sound psychological research; some philosophical ideas which help you, dear readers, reflect on your own lives and maybe consider adopting some of the processes and tools in a personally relevant and resonant way.

Alan B Jones

December 2017

Happiness

"The reason people find it so hard to be happy is that they always see the past better than it was, the present worse than it is, and the future less resolved than it will be."

Marcel Pagnol

I try to post some thought provoking quotes on my social media pages every day, frequently they are themed. Recently I shared a number of quotes from the 1960's TV show The Prisoner.

This was one of them ...

Give us information. You are then eligible for promotion perhaps more Where do you desire to go? What is your dream? I can supply it

Some casual readers of my posts possibly misunderstood and so I received several replies like these...

I wish to meet a kind loving sane man I can travel the world with and have my happy ending...please

I wish to win big on the Euro-Millions and build my dream home...please

I wish to become a multi-millionaire, but don't want to have to work in the USA

I want to get more people at my events, and promote bigger and better ones

I want to be a singer and perform in at BIG concerts, have loads of fans and earn lots of money

All of these 'dreams' were shared because the quote included the question 'what is your dream' and the apparent promise of being able to supply it.

I find it interesting that all of the wishes asked for were for things 'outside' of the individual and suggest that somehow the acquisition of 'a man', 'money', 'a dream home', a 'successful events company' and a large 'fan base' would bring about a transformation in the lives of those doing the wishing.

There were no questions as to 'how' or 'what' the individuals had to do themselves to manifest these changes - they were ok with the idea that someone else would be able to supply it.

One wonders if these people would, in time, become like the ex-millionaire I mentioned at the very start of this book?

If you were to ask one hundred people what they wanted in their lives almost all would probably say at some point 'happiness'.

But what makes people happy?

What brings you happiness?

Is money, relationships, family, career, achievements, success, health, time, space or the zillions of products our consumer-based society tell us are important? Or is it something else, less tangible, which we project on to these things.

Interestingly whilst every one of these items that could, possibly create happiness, they can also create the opposite.

Money-worries, Relationship-disasters, Family-problems, Career-Life balance and so on.

In Buddhist teachings, we hear that Dukkha (pain and suffering) is a consequence of our attachments to people, things and ideas.

The Eight-Fold Path is a system which is said to help reduce suffering and guess what, it all relies upon the actions of the individual.

These actions, or perhaps better thought of as attitudes, fall into three groups

Personal Wisdom

> **Right View** - the perspectives we have on the relationship between cause and effect

> **Right Resolve** - the nature of our intentions

Personal Actions

> **Right Speech** - how we tell our stories, communicate - the value of our words

> **Right Action** - the way we meet the challenges, our behaviours

Right Livelihood - the way we earn our living in terms of previously considered values

Personal Skills

Right Effort - in dealing with distractions and prevarications

Right Mindfulness - being aware of being aware

Right Concentration - being able to shift and focus attentions

Now those of my readers who are well versed in Buddhist teachings will immediately recognise my oversimplifications here as well as the (for the moment) lack of focus on spiritual or karmic issues. As far as this discourse is concerned we are exploring how this path or personal action and responsibility relates to the notion of happiness.

So, if the Eight-Fold path is about breaking out of continual cycles of pain and suffering, what do Buddhist say about happiness?

Well Happiness is one of the seven qualities which lead to and come from enlightenment - adherence to the eight-fold path.

These seven qualities are:-

Mindfulness - the seventh step on the eightfold path

Investigation - contemplation on the nature of reality

Energy - the ability to be energetic, a zest for life

Happiness - to realise that the craving for things outside of ourselves is the path of pain

Tranquillity - arising naturally from other qualities, it is the calmness of mind and body

Concentration - yes, the eighth step on the eightfold path

Equanimity - the balance between extremes; the middle path

His Holiness the 14th Dalai Lama has said,

"Happiness is not something ready-made. It comes from your own actions."

So, happiness is about what we do, not what we get.

Yet there are several self-help style books and gurus who seem to present happiness as something we have a right to; it is like a commodity that can be obtained if we look a certain way; wear a certain kind of clothing; which in turn attracts a certain kind of mate which defines a certain kind of life-style.

All of this is about material gain, rather than happiness itself.

"This planet has - or rather had - a problem, which was this: most of the people living on it were unhappy for pretty much of the time. Many solutions were suggested for this problem, but most of these were largely concerned with the movement of small green pieces of paper, which was odd because on the whole it wasn't the small green pieces of paper that were unhappy."

**Douglas Adams - Hitchhikers
Guide to the Universe**

You need to think carefully about what happiness is for you.

Research has shown that once some basic living needs are met and there is a small degree of financial security, an increase in terms of money (wealth) does not increase personal measures of 'happiness'. By the same token any relief of sadness obtained through 'retail therapy' is both short lived and can lead to personal recrimination for having 'wasted money'. As the gentleman in my opening story came to understand the 'things' that he thought brought happiness were projections, illusions created by what we are 'told' bring happiness.

In terms of focussing on long term financial gains, studies have shown that individuals often underestimate the time they spend on obtaining such gains, at the expense of other things which have no financial reward (family life and health for example). The end result is a generalised sense of unhappiness.

We also note from research that happiness is not achieved by simply repressing or avoiding the things that cause pain and burying them in overly positive affirmations.

By way of a direct example...

Don't think of a Pink Elephant...

The mind cannot process a negative, so simply trying to not think about the things we 'believe' make us unhappy is a pointless task.

The pink elephant proves it - right!

Dealing with pain and disappointment is something we will look at in the next section, so we'll say more there.

Practical keys to discovering your own happiness...

Well if we take note of what Buddhist teaching affirm, we need to develop a series of personal values, attitudes and practices which remind us of our own response-abilities. If tranquillity, peace of mind, focus and ability find a middle-path are considered as measures of, or even routes to, happiness then there must be something to consider there.

Mindfulness practices, as shown in numerous studies, are beneficial in terms of stress-reduction - stress, perhaps being a 'happiness killer'.

Psychologists who have been involved in the study of cognitive behaviourism have noted that 'attention' is a far more complex thing than we think it is. Where we place our attention, the unconscious processes which tell us what to 'pay attention to' and 'what to ignore' are important here.

In what is now a classic experiment observers were asked to watch a video of students throwing a ball. They were given the task of counting the number of times the student in the white T-shirt caught (or threw) the ball. At the end of the film observers were asked to report the number of throws/catches they had counted - most of the people were able to recount a number which matched the number in the film. They were then asked if they had seen 'the Gorilla' - almost everyone (around 95%) said 'no'.

When they were shown the video clip again, a short way into the sequence, a person in a Gorilla suit is seen to walk through the circle of catchers/throwers; stand in the middle, beat their chest, and walk off slowly.

This was not a trick - the 'gorilla' was there on the first viewing of the clip. However, because the focus of the activity was the counting of the catches/throws, the mind deleted the information that was 'the gorilla'.

Conscious Attention is a limited commodity. In a classic piece of work George Miller demonstrated that we can only pay conscious attention to between 5 and 9 'chunks' of information - the rest is processed unconsciously or even 'deleted' from your experience of the world.

Noting what you pay attention to in your surroundings, your work, your relationships is a good place to start considering what you are missing. A saying I use frequently, which I believe to be a 'truism' and stems from the research of cognitive behaviourists, is - *attention goes where emotion flows* and conversely *emotion flows where attention goes.*

So, if you are in a situation where you feel threatened, your attention will be directed towards possible sources of physical or emotional 'attack'. Your unconscious will select where to place your attention and you will be on 'high alert'. Such an internal state will affect what you see, hear, feel and understand

If you are aware of this possibility, you can allow yourself to direct your attention (consciously) elsewhere and so, perhaps, have a completely different perspective on the same situation.

In one experiment psychologists asked volunteers to end each day by creating a list.

One group were asked to list five events that had happened during the day; another group was asked to make a list of five things that annoyed them and a third group were asked to make a list of things they felt grateful for.

Follow-up questionnaires relating to feelings of 'happiness' and 'personal value' found that those who had made the list of things they were grateful for scored more highly than the other two groups.

What could be easier than creating your own daily 'gratitude list'?

Earlier it was suggested that 'retail therapy' produced a fairly short-term change in terms of 'being happy'. Well that is generally true, with one key exception.

The 'purchasing' of 'experiences' has a longer term 'happiness' factor than other forms of buying therapy. So, if you are going to spend, purchase those experiences which create positive, social emotional memories.

In a parallel study, it was found that engaging in Random Acts of Kindness also resulted in higher scores on personal measures of happiness, satisfaction and valuing of self.

Finally, then comes the notion that happiness is not an emotional state nor a commodity. It is a range of experiences, attitudes and practices which are reported to 'the self' as being happy. There are no limits to the amount of happiness and it is best considered as a personal journey, not a destination.

You are responsible for your own happiness, since it is about how you perceive yourself and your interactions with others and your environment. Other 'things' and 'people' can influence your immediate sense of happiness, but ultimately it about **you not getting in your own way** when it comes to your journey towards it.

Reiki Practitioners are taught Ushui's 'Just for Today' guidance...

Just for today

Do not get angry

Do not worry

Be grateful

Do a good days work without causing harm

Be kind to others

Those who are aware of the writings of Miguel Ruiz try to follow the Four Agreements...

Be Immaculate in Your Speech

Don't Make Assumptions

What other people think of you is no importance

You are always doing your best

Others may follow other metaphysical daily rituals for living or chivalric codes of ethics.

These codes encapsulate our values and approach to the world out there, but stem from a desire for inner peace, tranquillity and happiness.

HAPPINESS

1st Key to Exceptional Future Histories

Have a balanced attitude towards the acquisition of financial gain

Do not repress painful memories or situations

Practice Mindfulness

Explore where your attention drifts

Create a Gratitude List

Purchase Experiences

Engage in Random Acts of Kindness

Create (or follow) Your own Code of Daily Rituals

"Don't rely on someone else for your happiness and self-worth. Only you can be responsible for that. If you can't love and respect yourself – no one else will be able to make that happen. Accept who you are – completely; the good and the bad – and make changes as YOU see fit – not because you think someone else wants you to be different."

Stacey Charter

Stories

"Who are we but the stories we tell ourselves, about ourselves, and believe?"

Scott Turow

This is going to be an interesting set of ideas, which you may need a little time to get your head around. I'll list them so you can have an initial reaction and then we'll explore them in relation to creating your Future History.

The 'world' as you perceive it is really a largely personal construction of the 'real world' based upon information processed and 'coded' by your senses.

'Your world' as defined by your senses and constructed in your mind, is at least three steps removed from the 'World Outside' of you.

It can take as much as $1/10^{th}$ of a second for your brain to process sensory information; you are perceiving the world as it was $1/10^{th}$ of a second ago.

Our maps of reality, and the perceptions that construct them, are modified by our memories, associations, beliefs, values, emotions and language to name but a few.

Memories are reconstructions of associated events and are only as 'real' as the emotional lens you are currently viewing them through - they are malleable and selective.

Ok, have a think about those.

If you immediately say 'of course, I knew that', then you've probably been exposed to information and ideas developed by modern neuroscience - well done.

If you immediately say 'WHAT!!!', then allow me to guide you gently through this rabbit-hole of brain science.

BUT, before we go any further consider this.

If I present you with information that you already 'accept', then your physiology and internal responses could be described as being a comfortable nod, and the inner warmth of familiarity.

If I extend what you already know, by adding further information and conclusions, then you may get an 'ah ha' moment, typically associated with the 'ah ha' or equivalent internal dialogue and a smile.

If I further extend your knowing then we get to a 'Eureka' moment which is typified and an internal sigh of 'recognition', the eyes looking up-ward, and intake if breath and the explosion of 'the Eureka'.

It could be suggested that in all of the above cases you have not been introduced to anything new; your learning has just been extended.

However, If I present some information which is in total contradiction to what you already 'know' or are willing to accept then your physiology and internal processes could be described as a 'sigh' and downward nod of the head and perhaps the comment '*Bullshit!*'

I believe that it is on the borders of that *BS* response that we are more likely to learn something new. In some ways, the BS response is a reaction to previous learning being disrupted.

One of my favourite quotes is that *'most people think they are thinking, when they are simply rearranging their prejudices'*. Which is a provocative way of saying that information received by the brain is subjected to a pattern-matching, association based process which favours existing neural pathways.

So, the question has to be asked, what defines these 'existing neural pathways' and how can be we become more aware of our perceptual prejudices?

Ok, let's go back to the first few comments.

The way information gets from the 'outside' world to your brain is via your senses. Whilst we commonly think of the five senses of sight, hearing, taste, smell, touch, modern neuroscience has defined between 21 and 33 sensory processes in the body. However, sticking with the five for the moment...

Vision is really about light waves from the outside world, being focussed via the lenses of our eyes, turned into chemical reactions, which then produce electrical signals that are processed by the brain.

We cannot see all wavelengths of light and so our vision places limits on the natural world. The brain does not see pictures, but rather a series of electrical impulses which we understand as images.

Sound is about sound waves from the outside world, being focussed via the ear, turned into mechanical reactions (vibrations of hairs in the cochlear) which then produce electrical signals that are processed by the brain as hearing.

We cannot hear all frequencies of sound and so our hearing places limits on the natural world. The brain does not hear words, or sounds, but a series of electrical signals that are processed by the brain as sound.

I won't labour the point, but by extension you might be able to note how the same process applies to the other senses.

The reality is that we limit reality.

The reality is that we create internal representations of the world which is at least three steps removed from the reality being perceived,

Light Waves - Chemical Reactions - Electrical Signals

Visual Perception (Sight)

Sound Waves - Mechanical Reactions - Electrical Signals

Sound Perception (Hearing)

Some researchers have suggested that this process can take up to 1/10th of a second to complete, so our brains predict future events based upon previously experienced patterns to create the necessary illusion of working in 'real time'.

In his work Science and Sanity, Alfred Korzybski noted that **'the map was not the territory'**, which means that our internal maps of external reality are just that 'maps' - they are not the landscape of the real world, but our interpretations of it. More importantly, perhaps, is the idea that people do not respond to the world outside of themselves, but to their own internal maps of the world.

This is where the idea of stories comes in. Our personal map-making can be considered as personal myth-making. The stories we tell ourselves about our lives shape and reinforce our perceptual maps, and as mentioned in the last chapter, can become more responsible for what we pay most of our attention to.

Where do these stories come from?

First of all, there are the stories - the characters and themes - that stem from our culture. In this group of stories, we will find the archetypes (Heroine, Sage, Villain, Wizard. Wise Woman) and mythic themes (Questing, Finding Treasure, Otherworld Journeys) which Carl Jung and Joseph Campbell wrote widely about.

Other stories will come from the expectations, attitudes and responses to us as individuals from parents and peers. These may well be expressed as our confidence, or lack of; or self-worth, or lack of; self-esteem or lack of - and so on.

Adaptations to these stories will be written by our life experiences - early friendships, relationships, school, teachers, priests or spiritual leaders

These stories create an internal template about how the world works, our relationship to it and the people in it. As we create each new chapter in our personal stories there may well be repeating themes or incidents from which we create hard and fast rules about our ability to navigate life's challenges.

Whilst some of these stories may be revealed in dreams (or through psychoanalysis), many remain locked within our unconscious. They become the gatekeepers of new experiences, new input from the outside world, and so our attention will be focussed on those events which reinforce the pre-existing pathways; prejudices; beliefs and attitudes.

We may have to work hard to re-write some of the stories we have told ourselves even if we do recognise them.

You may have a personal story about how you are not worthy of being loved. Such a story may come from the way you were treated as a child. You may have a memory of ill-treatment, but perhaps do not fully understand the power of the story behind those memories.

As a character within this story you behave in ways which reinforce the role you have cast for yourself (again unconsciously). Your behaviours towards prospective partners may be seen as being 'needy'. Worse still, you may project the idea that such and such a person is 'needed' in order for you to be 'happy' and feel 'fulfilled'.

In a story like this, the potential partner is not an equal, but the source of everything that is required for you to be 'complete'. Such a story is unlikely to have a particularly happy ending, unless of course the prospective partner has cast themselves as 'rescuer' - in which, for a while at least, these co-dependent characters are having their immediate needs met.

It has been observed by many therapists that long-lasting relationships, can start out as being unequal in terms of needs and expectations, but that the individuals within those relationships co-write another story in which they are equals, with a shared journey.

To paraphrase Kahil Gilbran, the individuals become strong trees because they do not grow in each-others shadow.

Society can place expectations on individuals, so that its stories get mixed with personal stories. Consider the expectations or indeed the treatment of women at different times in Western culture and in different cultures today.

Religious teachings, art, literature, pornography, media - all of these can create shades and textures within the personal stories of women and men. Even the notions of extended or nuclear families; and life scripts of school, college, work, marriage, home, children play their part. If we feel that our life does not follow the story we tell ourselves, which in a large part is based upon the judgements of others, we may start to describe ourselves as being a failure.

These stories become our futures - 'I will always be clumsy and unattractive'. 'No one will ever like or care about me', 'All of my relationships will fail - because of me!'

Depressing isn't it.

But if you step back for a moment and remember that these are stories then, you could revise ad re-write them; even create empowering sequels - yes, create a future history!

You just need to recognise that the world you perceive and respond to is a representation of what your unconscious has selected to present to you and that the template it uses is based upon your beliefs, values, attitudes (which in turn have been derived from the stories you tell yourself).

"Hold On", I can hear you say, "wasn't all this about the nature of reality mentioned in the Buddhist stuff above?"

Yes, it most certainly was - Investigation is one of the seven qualities of enlightenment. Here you are not only being asked to consider the nature of reality and your perception of it, but the illusions created by the stories you have told yourself.

"Ok', you may now say. 'If these stories are not part of my conscious awareness, how do I know what to edit or re-write?'

That is a good point, however, the stories you tell yourself leave traces in the language you use on a daily basis.

For example, the words **'should'**, **'must'** and **'ought'** are command words. They imply someone is telling you (ordering you) to behave or think in a certain way.

"Little children **should** be seen and not heard", may have been a theme in your up-bringing, so your story contains beliefs about the value of what you have to say; the relevance of your feelings.

If your language, or self-talk, includes these words it is perhaps worth questioning 'who' is claiming that you 'should', 'must' and 'ought'?

When reflecting on an action stemming from a decision you have made, you find yourself saying 'I should have done this another way!", are you reflecting self-doubt and a story you hold about your own poor decisions making?

For example, you have chosen to have some 'you-time' and have a found a diversion that is relaxing, enriching and about YOU. Then, when you come to reflect on it, you find yourself saying "I should not have taken that time, I ought to have gotten on with some work" you may be negating the value of derived from that 'you time' and reflecting a story about being told that you must always be working, you are not worthy of the time you spend on your-self.

Using words like '**could**', '**may**', '**might**' actually imply an inner state of choice; these are words of possibility and so hint at personal stories that honour you and your decisions.

Another language pattern that can hint at a less than useful unconscious story is one which includes the generalisations of '**always**', '**every time**' and '**never**'...

For example -

"Every time I find someone I like, they let me down!"

"Men (women) always cheat on me"

Now it may be the case that every man (or woman) in your experience is unfaithful or that everyone you like lets you down. Is it as likely, however, that your personal stories (beliefs) are projecting certain kinds of expectations onto others and your attention is focussed on looking for examples of 'cheating' or 'failure to meet-up to your standards'?

What about this one ...

"Everybody hates me...!!!"

What do you think the story is there?

Now it is true that this kind of self-reflection requires a certain kind of approach. It is never about seeking to prove that your experience is 'wrong', it is about exploring other ways to consider the way you think about your experiences. Remembering that what you perceive is shaped by the stories you have been telling yourself and others have been reinforcing since you were a child. This is the kind of exploration that may best be undertaken with a professional guide (a coach or psychotherapist) but if that does not appeal to you there are some other possibilities.

Despite what some may believe about 'talking therapies' it has been shown that simply telling someone about your past issues and traumas, may not be as effective as might be thought. At worst the constant re-telling of traumatic stories keeps you locked into the traumatic experience - it reinforces the memory of it.

For this reason, professional therapists have tools which explore different ways of thinking about the stories they are being told. What has been shown to be useful if therapy does not appeal, is self-help based around writing about experiences. Indeed, evidence from research is that creative writing, and expressing feelings in diaries is beneficial.

So, if a professional talking cure is not to your taste, then a self-help writing cure can be useful. In my work, I often encourage clients to diarise, keep reflective journals (which includes the daily gratitude list mentioned above) all of which encourages self-reflection.

Self-Talk is, perhaps, the most important story-teller in your life. That little voice that either encourages you or dissuades you. If you listen to it you may hear echoes of your parents, teachers, childhood supporters or detractors; your own voice of doubt or affirmation. You can, believe it or not, converse with this voice and ask it to be more positive, more helpful. Using affirmations can, all other things being considered, encourage such a change.

It's the repetition of affirmations that leads to belief. And once that belief becomes a deep conviction, things begin to happen.
Mohammed Ali

What you say inside your head, will affect how you perceive and respond to the world.

Self-Talk can easily become limiting speech.

I can't do that?

I couldn't do that?

It's just impossible for me to undertake that challenge?

I'm just not good enough?

Again, think back to where those stories came from?

Each of these statements of impossibility can be reframed with one word. That word is 'YET'...

I can't do that – **yet.**

I couldn't do that – **yet**.

It is impossible for me to undertake that challenge – **yet.**

I'm just not good enough – **yet**.

It is the creation of possibility which encourages us to ask what needs to be done, what steps need to be taken, in order to meet that challenge. Then, like Ali, we are free to create a motivational mission statement. *'I am the greatest'*, may not be to your modest taste, but find something that resonates with you. Put this statement as the heading to the code of behaviour you created in the last section.

Your Mythic Journey

"People say that what we're all seeking is a meaning for life. I don't think that's what we're really seeking. I think that what we're seeking is an experience of being alive, so that our life experiences on the purely physical plane will have resonances with our own innermost being and reality, so that we actually feel the rapture of being alive."
Joseph Campbell

Who or What is a Hero?

In terms of literature and story the 'hero' is often the character who not only undertakes a perilous journey or quest, but the one who is 'changed the most' by that adventure.

In the Harry Potter tales, we may understand that it is Harry Potter who is the Hero since it is he who discovers his power, his heritage and is engaged in a battle with the evil Lord Voldemort. In that journey, inner questions as to his own heritage are raised.

However, we could just as easily see Neville as the ultimate Hero as it is he who, in that last battle, makes a valiant stand against overwhelming odds; it is he not Harry who rallies the almost defeated band of Hogwarts staff and students having transformed from a weakly, also-ran kind of character to a fully formed hero with a sword.

Joseph Campbell, writer and mythologist, noted that there seems to be a consistent structure to major mythic tales. In many ways, these stories can be seen as a built around three-key acts, phases or chapters.

Phase 1 (Chapter 1)

In general, terms the hero receives some news, or an insight which forces them to face a separation from their everyday life.

The fear of separation, of change, often means that the initial call to action is refused. Eventually, however, the lure of the challenge overcomes the inertia of the hero's desire to stay safe at home at which point a mentor appears to encourage the questor.

Phase 2 (Chapter 2)

The quest begins and there is a sense of descent into a world of chaos, or at least the unknown. Various challenges and tasks are presented which need to be overcome. Some of the solutions to these challenges require the development of special skills or talents; perhaps then acquisition of magical weapons or implements.

In the midst of these challenges there is either an implied or actual initiation into deeper 'truths' and mysteries. These in many ways are self-realisations as much as they are learnings; insights as much as they are rewards.

These ordeals faced and met, the hero seeks the road home. They have been fundamentally changed by the journey and may have the desire to remain in this 'other world' of magic, insight and renewal.

Phase 3 (Chapter 3)

The road home may not be without challenge, but the hero is impelled to return and share their story, their wisdom and sometimes the secret elixir which will enrich their people.

This concept was introduced by Joseph Campbell in The Hero with a Thousand Faces, who described the basic narrative pattern as follows:

A hero ventures forth from the world of common day into a region of supernatural wonder: fabulous forces are there encountered and a decisive victory is won: the hero comes back from this mysterious adventure with the power to bestow boons on his fellow man.

Whatever your 'past story', it is vital to remember that whilst **your past 'shapes you'**, it is **your future that 'defines you'**. Like a hero on a journey you move from challenge to challenge; situation to situation. In your adventure, there will be somethings within your 'control' and somethings clearly beyond the scope of your influence. You do, however, have choices about how you respond or behave.

The Mythic Cycle (which Campbell named a "monomyth") inspired Christopher Vogler in 1985 to produce a Disney Studio memo which described twelve stages of the hero's journey required to make a 'great story'.

1. The Ordinary World,

2. The Call to Adventure,

3. Refusal of the Call,

4. Meeting with the Mentor,

5. Crossing the Threshold to the "special world",

6. Tests, Allies and Enemies,

7. Approach the Innermost Cave

8. The Ordeal

9. Reward,

10. The Road Back,

11. The Resurrection

12. Return with the Elixir.

The Secret to Your FUTURE HISTORY

As part of the consideration of your own mythic journey we can consider each of these stages into a set of personal, reflective questions.

The Ordinary World
Where am I now?

The Call to Adventure
What are my challenges?

Refusal of the Call
What am I not considering?

Meeting with the Mentor
Who or what could guide me now?

Threshold to the "special world"
What are my dreams and intuitions?

Tests, Allies and Enemies
What challenges or trials am I facing at this moment?

Approach the Innermost Cave
What am I afraid of?

The Ordeal
How can I face my fears?

Reward
What rewards are there for succeeding?

The Road Back
What have I gained/learned?

The Resurrection
How have I changed?

Return with the Elixir
What can I now share?

You can ask these questions about any adventure you are currently experiencing and, indeed, those you are planning. In effect, you will be starting to re-write your own story in terms of where you are and where you want to be in YOUR future,

Carl Jung wrote widely on the nature and formation of archetypes. The Hero/Heroine are examples of archetypes, but so too are The Magician, The Trickster, The Sage, The Judge. Each of these can be thought of as exemplars, or ways to explore potential behaviours in response to challenges.

One of the most supporting and inspirational tools to achieve success is to have a hero. Oprah Winfrey, talk show host, once told Barbara Walters, renowned interviewer and newscaster, that, if it were not for Ms. Walters, she wouldn't be where she is today. This is a wonderful example of using a hero to achieve. The great thing about emulating heroes is that they can be living, dead or even fictitious.

Finding a hero (or heroine) to emulate gives you many achievement advantages. That person is already the success in the future you seek. Learn all you can about them. Find out what they purposefully did to achieve. What could they have done differently to make the process to success easier and faster? Keep a list of the person's traits that you wish to emulate, and incorporate them and anything that helped your hero/heroine to achieve into your plan of action.

You are not trying to 'copy' them, but understanding how they faced certain challenges may help you create your own personal resources.

It is all too often the case that when we face challenges our 'life script' or 'unconscious stories' restrict us from acting in different ways. We tend to have default positions, behaviours and practices - and if we do what we always have done we get the results we have gotten in the past!

STORIES

2nd Key to Exceptional Future Histories

Explore the basis for the stories you tell yourself.

Look at the beliefs that stem from these stories and ask how they limit your perception

Identify the language of limitation

Give your self-talk a talking to

Create a meaningful, personal mission statement

Ask yourself where you are in your current story

Identify Heroes/Heroines which can inspire you.

Imagine creative(heroic) responses to challenging situations

Motivation

People often say that motivation doesn't last.
Well, neither does bathing - that's why we recommend it
daily.

Zig Zigler

The word MOTIVATION implies movement.

We can define motivation as:

The desire an individual has to move from one position or
state of being, to another
AND
The behaviours which bring about that movement.

When looking at what motivates a person we can start by
looking at those things which drive (or, give power to) the
willingness to move from "state A" to "state B".

In order to better understand this, it is worth reflecting
upon the things which 'motivate' or drive you towards the
things you want to achieve and those things (stories, ideas,
behaviours, attitudes, values) which fuel your change and
those which 'block' your progress.

Everything a person says, thinks and does is motivated by
something inside of their conscious or unconscious mind. It
has been said that everything we do is motivated by something
- fear, hunger, the desire for self-fulfilment. In very simple

terms the need for survival (both personal and of the species) motivates us as individuals in very obvious ways; ways we'd sometimes prefer to ignore perhaps.

There are processes that operate at a very basic level within the human animal. Evolutionary Psychology, a relatively new area of study, seeks to match behaviours to an evolutionary drive or motivation. Some very interesting work has been done on the nature of sexual attraction, male and female roles and so on.

It was Maslow who identified a hierarchy of 'needs' and the suggestion is that the human animal is motivated to engage in behaviours which seek to have them met.

Based on Maslow's Hierarchy of Needs

Spiritual Needs
Self Empowerment
Aesthetic Needs
Knowledge & Understanding
Esteem Needs
Need to Belong
Safety Needs
Physiological Needs

This 'pyramid' is well known and to Maslow's original five-stages more recent thinkers have added a spiritual (or at least transpersonal level). Obviously, these authors have a personal world view which recognises the importance of spirituality.

In terms of Maslow our needs are met in a kind of hierarchical manner. Our first need relating to physical survival and only once that is assured will the other 'need' become an aspiration or goal.

Our behaviour is directly linked the meeting of these needs.

Three things become apparent immediately, the first is how the individual *knows* when some of these needs have been met; the second how we set about meeting these needs and thirdly any cultural issues that become linked with these needs.

Dreikurs was a psychologist and educator who looked at behaviour in learners. He suggested that human misbehaviour is the result of feeling a lack of belonging to one's social group. When this happens the individual acts from one of four "mistaken goals": undue attention, power, revenge or avoidance (inadequacy).

Driekurs was influenced another psychologist and psychotherapist, Adler, whose key contribution to the world of therapy was a recognition of the importance of an individual's interaction with society and the concept of the 'inferiority complex'.

It is important to recognise that each of the psychological ideas explored so far are teleological in nature - a fancy way of saying that there is some final goal, destination or purpose towards which we move.

In Maslow, there is the idea of achieving Self-Actualisation; in Dreikurs and Adler the idea of becoming a whole, balanced individual.

All of these approaches presuppose some kind of destination (goal) or idea of completion which may well simply reflect philosophical ideals defined by a particular culture at a particular time.

When translated into therapy, education and coaching there is the idea that people are motivated to attain specific goals with the recognition that they will have personal attitudes, values and understandings of the details of their final goal.

Sound confusing?

Well it's not only about understanding the goal (or dream); it's about recognising the all that achieving that goal requires.

The Five Step Motivational Model

A couple of years ago I was honoured to be invited to deliver a Key Note address at the Sport's Conference – a superb event which was very well attended. I was sharing the 'platform', as it were, with their first key note speaker Talan Skeels-Piggins.

What can I say?

Not only was this man's story inspiring and inspirational; it was moving and motivational and, as a speaker, very difficult to follow.

For those not in the know, Talan was a member of the 2010 UK Paralympic downhill skiing team. He told his personal story of triumph over adversity starting in 2003 when he was involved in a horrific motorbike accident which shattered his spine and broke his neck, leaving him paralysed from the chest down.

His description of the accident and the aftermath had his audience horrified, amazed and amused. If you get the chance to hear Talan speak then please take advantage of the opportunity.

During his talk, I was not only as moved as the rest of the audience, but because I knew I had to follow his presentation, was forced to reflect more immediately on what he was saying. I remembered being in a similar situation having to 'follow' the Falklands veteran Simon Weston and a broad generalisation struck me.

It seems that it is only after a major life trauma, when we, as human beings, take very careful stock of what it is we really want to achieve. When we are introduced to our mortality we have to take stock of what is important and valuable to us.

I recalled one of my early teachers/trainers asking the group I was in the following question:-

"If you were given only eighteen months to live what you would you do?"

The instructor left the room and we all chatted about his question. At first we started to think of maxing-out credit cards; taking out loans and doing all of the 'fun things' we could imagine.

After a few moments, we all quietened to create a list of quite mundane things really - to visit certain places, to create something, to make the most of our families and friends.

When the tutor returned he asked us to read our 'bucket list' out. We all listened to each other and thought about what was being said. Then we were all asked one sobering question...

"If these are things you want to achieve, why are you all waiting until you're nearly dead to do them?"

It was a real "Dead Poets Society" moment, *"Captain Oh, My Captain...."*

Both Talan and Simon describe their feelings after the events that shaped their lives as being those of anger, frustration, depression - a sense of 'why me?'

Both Talan and Simon described a 'turning point' after which something 'inside' clicked and gave them a new direction, a new focus.

Both Talan and Simon then engaged in what could be described as a focussed course of actions (behaviours) that led them from where they 'were' to where they 'wanted to be'. So, what can we learn about motivation from their stories?

Firstly - it is about accepting CHANGE – having some feelings about that change and more importantly looking beyond the fear, uncertainty and resistance to that change into some alternative future.

Secondly - it is about CONTROL – psychologists talk about LOCUS of CONTROL. Individuals with a 'high locus of control' will make themselves responsible for their own actions. Those with a 'low locus of control' will tend to put responsibility for change onto other people and situations.

In both Simon and Talan's case their accidents were completely out of their control. This means that the resulting physical limitations where also out of their control.

They became 'motivated', for want of a better term, when they started to focus on the things they could control and take responsibility for.

Thirdly - it is about the 'NEED" for a 'DREAM' an aspiration or a target.

The popular book The Secret takes sound psychological and behavioural advice and turns it into what we could see as a 'psuedo-mystical' belief system. In some ways, the 'handing over to the Universe could be seen as a handing over of personal responsibility. But as Talan, specifically noted, the idea of having a dream and surrounding himself with images that reminded him of his 'goal' was very motivational. Hence noting the value of 'dream' or 'vision' boards.

Fourthly - there is the need to work back from the dream in order to identify the STEPS that need to be taken from the NOW which lead into the FUTURE.

In education, we have spent so much time thinking about motivation rather than being motivational that we forget the real value of what have been called SMART targets.

Simple Statement of outcome with a Measure linked to success, based upon...

Achievable and Realistic steps set within a valid Time frame.

Whilst many of you who have heard me speak on the topic of motivation know that I think this model can be improved, I feel that the value of stating goals in terms of steps, timescales and measures is essential to getting where you want to go.

Fifthly - it is about celebrating any success that is a *'step in the right direction'*. Such celebrations are reminders that there is a journey and that there have been changes. These celebrations will also allow for review and reflection so ensuring that the 'goal' remains valid and relevant.

What the stories told by Simon, Talan and many many others tell us is that motivation comes from emotional connection to a goal; a willingness to take control of what you can; to be responsible for your own future and having the strength to bring your behaviours in line the steps you have identified.

It's about D+PMA+A

Dream + Positive Mental Attitude + Application

In summary then, the Five Step Motivational Model defines...

Step 1 CHANGE – having some feelings about that change and more importantly looking beyond the fear, uncertainty and resistance to that change into some alternative future.

Step 2 CONTROL – knowing that there are things you can have a direct influence on and those you can't (yet).

Step 3 the 'NEED" for a 'DREAM' an aspiration or a target.

Step 4 identify the STEPS that need to be taken that will create the FUTURE.

Step 5 CELEBRATE any success that is a 'step in the right direction'. Such celebrations are reminders that you are on a journey and that there have been changes. These celebrations will also allow for review and reflection so ensuring that the 'goal' remains valid and relevant.

So, you have an empowering goal, a dream or an ambition - and you've thought about these five steps, but what's next?

The challenge for many people is not the lack of ambitions, nor perhaps even the emotional desire for those dreams. It is in the practicalities of making these dreams happen; to have the ability to create their future history. If my observations about Simon, Talan and my fellow students are correct, then sometimes we fail to take the clear steps into our dream future until something forces us - until the situation presents itself - until tomorrow, and of course tomorrow never comes.

Until one is committed, there is hesitancy, the chance to draw back. Concerning all acts of initiative (and creation), there is one elementary truth, the ignorance of which kills countless ideas and splendid plans: that the moment one definitely commits oneself, then Providence moves too. All sorts of things occur to help one that would never otherwise have occurred. A whole stream of events issues from the decision, raising in one's favour all manner of unforeseen incidents and meetings and material assistance, which no man could have dreamed would have come his way. Whatever you can do, or dream you can do, begin it. Boldness has genius, power, and magic in it. Begin it now."

This is a great quote and one which can inspire us here. We often find it in sources referencing The Secret or texts on Cosmic Ordering since it can be read to imply the Cosmos, Universe or Providence falls in line with the commitment to our goal. This is, perhaps, as erroneous as the attribution of the quote.

The quote is often attributed to Goethe, a particular genius 18th Century genius. However extensive research by the Goethe Society have found no German references to this text.

The *"Until one is committed..."* quotation is in fact by William Hutchinson Murray (1913-1996), from his 1951 book entitled The Scottish Himalayan Expedition. The actual final lines from W.H. Murray's book end this way...

"...which no man could have dreamed would have come his way. I learned a deep respect for one of Goethe's couplets:

"Whatever you can do, or dream you can do, begin it. Boldness has genius, power, and magic in it!

And it is doubtful whether Murray's attribution of the final lines is from Goethe. The point I am trying to make is that whatever the source of the quotation, we can interpret it in terms of all that you have already read in this book.

The moment we truly commit ourselves to a goal, and provided we have dealt with all of our stories of hesitation, our own psychology starts to drive our perception to notice what has been unnoticed previously.

It all goes back to attention and where, emotionally, we place it.

Imagine for a moment, your freezer breaks down. What happens, apart from the panic about where to put all of your frozen goods?

You recall information about where to get freezers repaired or replaced.

All those advertisements you have been exposed to for months suddenly make sense, they come to mind, because now there is an emotional need.

You buy a new car, well at least new to you, and choose a rather unusual make, model or colour because you want to be 'unique'.

The moment you drive off the forecourt you see other examples of that car - that specific, make, model and colour!

Now it could be that the Cosmos has listened to your needs and answered you by creating just what you want. It could be, but is it possibly more reasonable to recognise, that your perception has become attuned to your emotional need and you notice those things that are of (immediate) interest?

In his book The Luck Factor, Richard Wiseman noted that people who believed they were lucky, had lucky routines or tokens, appeared to have more 'luck'. His conclusion, and one that is worth considering, is that the *luck-mind-set* correlated to people who were willing to take risks!

It was the willingness to seek opportunities and take a chance that generated the experience that some would call 'luck'.

This is not to dismiss the existence of lucky-breaks or fate dealing a fortuitous hand, but it is about having a mind-set of being willing to 'take risks' or 'going with the gut'. This of course implies that we have personal stories about it being OK to trust ourselves to take a chance, or if these stories are not in our direct experience, consider how our heroes may have behaved.

Putting all of this together as a useable framework may seem like a major challenge. However, from what we have learned so far, we can find our way through this with relative ease

We need to believe we can achieve our dreams...

We need a compelling emotional vision...

We need to ensure that vision is in line with our personal codes of values and attitudes...

We need a plan!

SMART targets as mentioned above are often presented as being that plan but I believe they are **inherently de-motivational**.

Consider ...

A **SIMPLE** statement of desired outcome - yes this makes perfect sense since it allows for a compelling vision...

A **MEASURABLE** outcome - yes, again essential as it is important to define fully the destination...

And here is where the problem lies.

ATTAINABLE and **REALISTIC** - are these not the same thing? If something is attainable then it's probably realistic and vice versa.

TIME-BOUND - ok, so we do need 'deadlines' and 'time scales'

Close to twenty years ago now, I was using the SMART frame, and found that it lacked any reference to what I have now defined as the Five Step Motivation Model (above). Also, in NLP terms, a SMART target is not a *well-formed outcome*. A well-formed outcome needs to meet the following criteria...

The Goal (Outcome) needs to be described in sensory based terms (more about this later).

It needs to have a clear set of steps and a time frame for completion.

It needs to be ecological, in that it meets the values, attitudes and future needs of the individual.

SMART targets only meet one of the three criteria.

So, let me introduce **SMARTER** targets, a framework I've been using in education and with clients for two decades and which I now hear quoted back at me.

When creating a target, goal or ambition here are the SMARTER steps and the key questions which make it work.

SIMPLE - statement of goal, target or ambition.

What do you want to achieve?

Describe it as clearly as you can

Can you state your dream in simple terms so that it can be understood by others?

MEASURABLE - simply knowing when you've achieved the goal

How will you know when you've attained your goal?

What measures of success will you personally use?

ACHIEVABLE - what are the steps towards your goal?

Can you identify clearly the steps you need to take from the now to your future?

At each step what will you need to do, learn, organise?

Can you clearly identify the resources you need for each step?

REWARDING - what will you get out of this?

What are the emotional gains for achieving this goal or target?

What are the practical gains for achieving this goal or target?

How will achieving this goal, target, ambition satisfy you?

EFFECT - what will be the effects of achieving this?

What will be the practical results of achieving this goal?

What broader impacts will achieving this goal have on you?

What broader impacts will achieving this goal have on those around you?

What will change when you achieve the goal, target, ambition?

REVIEW - how will you review progress and celebrate achievements?

How will you keep a track of your progress?

How will you ensure after achieving each step that your goal is still valid?

When you have achieved this what will this enable you to do?

What will you do next?

The more detail with which these questions, and others that you will create, can be answered the clearer your goal, target or ambition will become - and, more importantly, the clearer each step towards your goal will be.

It's not the goal itself that is important in terms of 'making it happen', but the reflection needed to write the goal down in this detail.

In considering the questions within the SMARTER framework, you will be not only considering the resources and skills required to achieve the goal, but also the consequences of doing such. More importantly this will require a consideration of your own needs and values. If you have considered carefully the above section on Happiness, you may have already noted some shifts in what you believe you actually need and desire.

Simply setting a goal and handing it over to the Universe can mean that you fail to own any responsibility for it. Research has shown that successful goal setting is about the degree of self-efficacy and control of own achievement the individual has. To treat the whole process in terms of simplistic wish creation misses the whole point of making 'you' a creator of your future history.

When I started an aspect of my own journey that involved a study of esoteric and magickal traditions I remember something my then, *guru*, said in a session.

A member of the circle asked if he could use 'magick' ('spells', or 'prayers') to get him a well-paid job.

The teacher laughed and said...

"Yes, but getting off your arse, smartening yourself-up and applying for the kind of jobs you want is far quicker and easier!"

MOTIVATION

3rd Key to Exceptional Future Histories

Create goals which deserve your attention

Be active in the creation and execution of your targets

Describe your gaols, targets and dreams in exquisite detail

Consider the changes success will bring to you

Once you have created **SMARTER** targets as above consider writing your dreams using the following template...

SIMPLE

MEASUREABLE

AWESOME

RIDICULOUS

TIME-BOUND

EFFECT(ive)

REVIEW(ed)

Decisions

"What lies behind us and what lies before us are tiny matters compared to what lies within us."
Ralph Waldo Emerson

We have attempted to explore some of the keys to creating personal future histories.

If our goal is 'happiness', then we've considered the idea that this is a quality we have that comes from self-knowledge. It is not necessarily a temporary feeling that shifts with our emotional tide, it is rather a state of being that includes tranquillity (inner peace) and a sense of being in-tune with yourself and your Universe.

We then looked briefly at the stories we tell ourselves, their origins. The notion that the voices in our heads building us up or bringing us down are the legacies of our past. Our stories shape not only the way we look at the world, but the way we act within it.

In the last section, we considered being moved-into-action, or being motivated; attention goes where emotion flows and what we pay attention to can become the focus of our energy.

Your future history stands on these three legs. What you now choose to do shapes what you become.

'Your decisions, or lack of decisions, determine the reality of your life' If we do not take responsibility for how we live, life will feel unfair and oppressive. Making a decision not to live like this anymore is to realise that, at last, we can choose our life's direction – and this brings a feeling of empowerment.

Unknown

White Wolf Inspirations & Wise Words For You

Make no mistake you are **always** making decisions.

Some decisions may be conscious, considered and based upon reflection.

Some decisions may be unconscious, driven by an immediate need to act and truly impulsive.

Some decisions are deferred, the decision has been to make no decision

Read those last three sentences again only change the word 'decisions' for the word 'choices'. How did that feel to you?

Does the change of wording alter the emotional impact or relevance in any way?

If we revisit the information about the brain and perception in the chapter on Stories, we can make another possibly shocking statement. Since you are only conscious of that which your unconscious mind shares and since we do not fully know what that part of our mind deletes (edits) then all decisions (choices) are based upon the programming (stories, beliefs, prejudices, experiences) of our past.

True Free Will is a delusion which stems from our personal illusions of reality!

It is for this reason that so many philosophical teachings and schools of mystery teachings spend so much effort in encouraging their students to consider deeply the relationships between the concepts of self and the world that "self" inhabits.

"A human being is a part of the whole called by us universe, a part limited in time and space. He experiences himself, his thoughts and feeling as something separated from the rest, a kind of optical delusion of his consciousness.

This delusion is a kind of prison for us, restricting us to our personal desires and to affection for a few persons nearest to us.

Our task must be to free ourselves from this prison by widening our circle of compassion to embrace all living creatures and the whole of nature in its beauty."

Einstein

A full discussion of this point is perhaps not relevant here, save for the intention of reminding you to engage fully in a personal exploration of own stories and your motivations.

What is also relevant here is that even if we do not have 'true free will', we still need to make decisions (choices) about who and where we'd like to be. The more considered these choices then, perhaps, the clearer the path and the more influence we have on how external events impact on us.

Marcus Aurelius, the soldier, poet and Stoic philosopher, noted that events are simply events and it is the individual who gives them meaning. Aurelius was echoing the ideas of Stoic philosophers before him and presenting us with a very clear challenge about how we interpret things that happen around us.

I may be driving my car; get 'cut-up' by another driver, and experience rage.

That rage is my emotional reaction to the actions of another and I may, in telling others, state that this other driver 'made me angry'.

No, he did not, my reaction was anger (which may or may not be justified), but **it is my anger and I have to deal with it**.

I can abdicate that responsibility, calling it blame, but it is how I feel 'now' that requires me to take some kind of action.

Where we focus our attention, our emotions and our actions create the definition of any event. The events are not you, but they can impact upon you. The degree of that impact is more about the personal relevance you place on the event rather than the event itself.

Remember shit happens - things will disrupt your personal peace and tranquillity and your path towards it.

Bad things happen to Good people, and Good things happen to Bad people. Yet note that even here we are giving a value of good or bad to an event or indeed a person - such a value is a personal judgement. If you accept that things can disrupt your plans, then you can be flexible in your responses rather than spending time and effort trying to hallucinate the cosmic reasons for the shit!

Remember, what is shit to some is fertiliser to others!

Some of this goes back to the idea of 'locus of control' as discussed in motivation, but here we are being asked to consider the decisions and choices we can make regardless of what the world offers us in the way of resistance, feedback or support. Whether times are 'good' or 'bad' we can still choose how to respond.

When we feel we have no choices, then we need to look again and create some!

In all of this we must remember that there is a difference between a 'reason' and an 'excuse'. In my experience, a number of people claim 'reason' when they mean 'excuse'. The dictionary tells us that ....

A **Reason** - is a cause, explanation, or justification for an action or event.

An **Excuse** - an attempt to lessen the blame attaching to (a fault or offence); try to justify.

A reason presupposes that that are clearly identifiable explanations whereas an excuse <u>alludes</u> to a possible set of identifiable explanations.

"Sorry I am late the traffic was horrendous'

This could be taken to be a good reason, especially if the person apologising is rarely late and a good time-keeper. However, if the reality is that the individual overslept and was forced to catch a later bus at a busier time, then perhaps it's a reasonable sounding excuse (invoking possible causes) but is, nevertheless, an attempt to shift responsibility for one's own tardiness.

How many of the reasons you give for not starting a project, or a plan or a path-towards a desired future are actually excuses?

We lie to ourselves because such lies satisfy the stories that have shaped us, rather than those which will define us. So, we defer decisions and actions which could take us forward by creating a whole host of 'reasons' as to why now is not the right time. If not now - then when will the time ever be right?

A number of years ago I was asked to sort through some old papers from a local society in order to write a history of that community group. I was given permission to use any notes, scribblings, agendas and minutes I found to write the groups story. Amongst the papers I found this poem and I have shared it with several workshop groups since.

Of all the sad, sad words that pass men's lips,
The saddest of them all is these — "It might have been"
It might have been — It might have been
Four little words, yet what do they mean?
They tell us of misery, ruin and loss,
Of the fortune that's gone on the turn or the toss
Of a card or a coin

They tell of the dear ones gone pass recall
A memory now though she once was his all.
It might have been.
Of shame and repentance and who knows but you
In the depths, your heart holds memories too...
Memories, memories, shattered cracked dreams
Broken forever.
Things that once had been secure in your grasp.
Now well, they might have been
They pass ever before us in ghastly array,
Their skeleton chains rattle by day,
And worse in the night they come back to torment us,
To mock and to say,
"We're the ghosts of your promises your hopes and your dreams
We're the things that you worked for,
Your plans and your schemes.
We're far away from you
There's a gulf in between,
We're gone now forever,
But once might have been".

I have tried to search for the author of these words and have found that the phrase "*For of all sad words of tongue or pen The saddest are these: "It might have been!* come from a poem by John Greenleaf Whittier (1807–1892) called Maud Muller.

It may be that this bitter-sweet poem by Whittier inspired the writer of the pages I found in a cellar, in a trunk, in a community hall, in Cornwall.

Perhaps, but what matters is that these words, whatever their true source, can and do reach out from the past to inspire our individual futures.

One last thing to think about here - prevarication!

This is a great word and is something we are all guilty of. It's about putting off (creating reasons or excuses) for not taking action.

For many people prevarication isn't about inaction, in fact it takes a lot of effort to prevaricate. If you consider prevarication as 'creative avoidance', then you may be able to reflect upon it a little more.

Here's a great example of creative avoidance...

You 'want' to complete your accounts which you store on your computer - but first you decide to check your emails; which leads you to follow a link to a Facebook page; which leads you to read someone's 'status update; which 'forces you' to make a comment; to which someone replies so you comment back...

All of these things have a value and a purpose, but perhaps after an hour of so 'lost' in the world of the Internet, you come back to thinking about your accounts – however, first you now need a tea-break.

We're all guilty of this kind of avoidance. A task which we are 'not looking forward' to is relegated lower and lower in a list of things that, well, you actually would possibly need to do - but not yet!

It has been suggested that the 'average' person has five social media accounts and spends up-wards of two hours a day on managing them. These figures rise for people who are self-employed as social media is seen as being an important marketing platform. (Yes, and in looking all of that up I've managed not to start my accounts!)

Here are two tips I share with businesses and individuals about tackling those tasks which need to be done, but induce creative avoidance.

1) Take a stop watch and set it to countdown five minutes. Determine to give yourself those five minutes focussed on the doing the task. Not preparing to do it - actually doing it. When the stop-watch chime rings make a decision as to whether this is a good place to leave what you have started.

Here's the thing. Our psychology is such that once a task is started we tend not to want to leave it incomplete or at a point that is not easy to return to (a natural break). This five minutes serve to put you into the space to continue. It also means that you have made that start!

2) The D.D.D. Approach to correspondence, emails and tasks. We will have daily routines as to the checking of emails, correspondence and so on. Because the technology involved in communications these days is instant, we have fallen into the

trap of needing to be instantaneous in our responses, In the 'old days' technology served us, not us it.

So, you could decide that emails, for example, are checked twice or three times a day only. When checking them you can then apply the following approach...

> **DEAL** immediately with all of these requiring a simple reply, acknowledgement or easily found piece of information
>
> **DUMP** all of those items that you know you won't ever read, even though you say you will
>
> **DEFER** all of those items requiring a considered response to a **defined** later time.

(In businesses where you are managing a team the approach could be written as Deal, Dump, Delegate)

Remember your time is your time, and it is valuable. You can make decisions on how that time is used. Time is a finite commodity - whether we like it or not, there are only so many hours in the day; so many days in a month and so many months in a year.

Some people have spent thousands of pounds in attending time management seminars; buying the latest time keeping software and so on. The answer to time management is simple - dominoes.

Identify the tasks you need to do and give them a meaningful timescale (yes, we're back to the SMARTER framework again) and visualise them as dominoes. You can then organise these dominoes in a line, prioritising the tasks.

I know I know, I have been accused of having a very 'male-mind' in this regard - perhaps so. The reason, however, that these tasks are dominoes, is that I can choose to re-think the order of the dominoes, which ones are crucial (maybe they can be visualised as being 'red') and which ones are fixed points on a timeline. I sometimes consider the dominoes to be of slightly different sizes or thicknesses depending on the length of time I think each will take to complete (remove from the line).

It isn't rocket science is it!

Things will either get done or they won't, you will create the time or you won't but if you accept that any task can be reduced to a series of steps (mini-dominoes) then maybe this technique will help keep you focussed. More relevantly the process requires you to reflect on those things which are really important to you and which are simply distractions you can choose to enjoy.

DECISIONS

4th Key to Exceptional Future Histories

Reflect on the decisions you have made in the past - but don't get stuck there!

Recognise that not making a decision is a decision in itself

Reflect upon your REASONS for not taking action

Challenge your EXCUSES for not taking action

Notice your own patterns of prevarication (creative avoidance)

Be responsible for and to your own decisions

Shifting

"All successful men and women are big dreamers. They imagine what their future could be, ideal in every respect, and then they work every day toward their distant vision, that goal or purpose."

Brian Tracy

So, here's the deal...

You have a dream, an ambition a goal. In fact, you have had dreams, ambitions and goals before BUT you've never really had the success you wanted.

What went wrong?

Well the first thing to really think about is how YOU might be hijacking your own success.

Think what could be getting in your way?

May I offer some questions for you to consider.

Do you REALLY want what you dream?

We all have dreams, ambitions, desires and hopes but the reality of the things we wish for may be somewhat removed from the ideal which we imagine.

Dreams of wealth and fame are one thing, but the reality of those things may be something different. Unless you ask the question, WHAT WOULD BE DIFFERENT when I have achieved my goal and honestly reflect upon the 'pros' and 'cons' there is a possibility that the "unconscious self" will sabotage 'conscious action' so leading to frustration.

Have you REALLY planned for it?

This is more than just having a destination. It is about having a map of the journey.

This map needs to highlight the way-points, the pit-stops and the comfort breaks.

Recognise that goals change and dreams can evolve and that the journey itself is important.

Have you OPENLY STATED what you want?

Committing to a particular course of action, to a specific journey, in your own mind is one thing. Writing it down, promoting it and telling other people is something else. I will leave you to decide which is the more valuable in supporting you on your journey.

Have you PREPARED for SUCCESS?

Preparing for success is about creating a vision of the 'future you' that is so complete that you can start to anticipate how other things will change around you – that includes not only your behaviour but also the reactions and behaviours of others. Speak to anyone who has won a large amount on a lottery and you will understand how this works.

Are your VALUES and ATTITUDES in line with your dream?

So, you may desire something; you may dream about it and you may well start working towards it. If your internal values, personal attitudes and emotional compass are not in-line with what you are 'becoming' or 'will become' then you are on a path that will not bring happiness. If you have to sacrifice what you feel makes you in order to achieve a stated goal you are setting up stressful internal conflicts that may be difficult to resolve or reconcile.

Are you FRIGHTENED about living your dream?

In other words, does success scare you?

This fear may come beliefs you have about your worthiness to succeed or from the thought that you will be moving away from what you know, what you are comfortable with.

It may sound obvious and a little 'trite' but CHANGE is the only CONSTANT in the universe. Change brings with it uncertainty and doubt. It often requires you to step away from the comfort zone of what you know and who you know. There are many people who prefer to stay trapped within their comfort zone when faced with major, personal, life changing choices.

Thinking about these questions forces you to decide if what you dream is really your dream and helps better prepare you for total commitment to your future success.

If you have been following the thoughts so far in this book these questions, and possible ways to answer them, have already been presented. We will deal with the notion of change in the next section, but now we need to consider how we can turn our SMARTER goals and ambitions into a FUTURE HISTORY.

Everything we have considered prior to this point has been a prelude to what I will share here. The following will join some dots and emphasise the reflections that have gone before are vital to your success - **a success which you own**.

Thinking back to our role model, Muhammed Ali, we discovered that he seemed to 'predict' the outcome of his fights and, for a number, he was correct, in his predictions. Now either he had some kind of 'psychic' gift, or more likely he had a skill of creating empowering, practical visions of the future.

Ali claimed the reason behind all of his success was due to visualizing victory prior to a fight and imagining himself celebrating a win in front of an arena full of fans days before the fight. More importantly he did not rely on this technique, he understood his potential and worked hard to achieve it. In his own words ...

"I hated every minute of training, but I said, 'Don't quit. Suffer now and live the rest of your life as a champion.'"

He further stated ...

The fight is won or lost far away from witnesses - behind the lines, in the gym, and out there on the road, long before I dance under those lights.

So, his future visioning was used to keep his attention and emotions on his stated goal.

There is a generally accepted notion that the brain (mind) at a functional level cannot tell the difference between the real and the imagined.

This simple assertion has led to some rather extravagant claims by some writers in the self-help movement, but the evidence is that mental rehearsal linked to physical rehearsal improves performance - increases success. In some ways, this does seem at odds with other research which suggests that visualising bright outcomes may not actually lead to achievement. Well, if you've been following our journey to this point, you will quickly see what **visualisation alone isn't going to cut it.**

SMARTER targets define the goal (dream) and ask you to consider the effects of achievement of that goal, but unless you have explored the stories which have shaped you, you may not bring a balanced emotional energy (motivation) to its attainment.

The secret to creating empowering visualisations, FUTURE HISTORIES, lies in a way of thinking about how the brain constructs meaning. What follows is best considered as a metaphor for what happens, and an oversimplified one at that, but it does create a useable framework for our purposes.

The process I am about to describe I call SHiFTing, and is based upon ideas from the field of Neuro-Linguistic Programming (NLP).

One of the key ideas in NLP, based upon the notion that we construct personal realities, is that we 'code' experience in terms of four-key 'inputs' - vision, hearing, kinaesthetic (feelings) and meta-cognition (thinking). In NLP texts these are referred to as V (visual) A (auditory) K (kinaesthetic) and Aid (Auditory-Digital - self-talk).

For the sake of ease, we can consider these elements being SEEing, HEARing, FEELing and THINKing.

Hence SHiFTing!

NLP practitioners maintain that any experience can be coded (experienced and recalled) using these 'modalities'. Think about a nice, positive memory now - something that you have experienced.

You can describe that memory in terms of what you SAW, HEARD, FELT and THOUGHT.

There's more. NLP techniques frequently include the 'manipulation' of these modalities by inviting those they are working with to make the pictures, bigger and bolder; the sounds louder; the feelings more intense and the self-talk about that moment more prominent.

If, rather than recalling a positive experience, the client recalls a more challenging memory, then the intensity of the components (SHFT) can be reduced.

Now whilst the therapy aspects of NLP are beyond the scope of this book, the practical applications for goal setting are not.

You may remember that when I spoke about targets in a previous section I mentioned the idea of a well-formed outcome.

One of the conditions of a well-formed outcome was the use of sensory based descriptions of the goal or target. The See, Hear, Feel, and Think framework allows you to create such a sensory based description of what, to all intents and purposes, is a future history.

The framework can be used by asking the following questions...

When you have achieved your goal what would you SEE yourself doing?

When you have achieved your goal what would you HEAR yourself and others saying?

When you have achieved your goal what would you be FEELING?

When you have achieved your goal what would you be THINKING (saying to yourself)?

It is very easy to treat this exercise with a degree of flippancy and this does little to create a motivational future history. For this framework to be of value you need to create a thorough and complete set of answers to these questions. Let's look at each in turn and see how this works.

What would you SEE yourself doing?

Describe in detail your future history, see it big and bright as if you are looking through your own eyes. What would you be seeing; the details of the situation.

Notice how your posture, your body language would appear to someone watching you, how would you be breathing?

Notice how you would be dressed, your appearance, your 'bearing' and demeanour.

What would you HEAR?

This is not simply about the sound and the quality of the sound, it is about the words you would hear. Make a list of the things you would hear others say about your achievement; the way you'd be speaking to others in your visualisation.

Notice tones of voice, pacing and way words are being said.

Notice the sounds of the surroundings you would be finding yourself in.

What would you be FEELING?

This is not simply about using single words to describe your feelings, but about unpicking the details of the feelings.

Where in your body are these feelings?

What are the qualities of these feelings?

A much more difficult set of questions, but these feelings can be described in terms of location (in the body), intensity and type. They can also be described in terms of metaphor - their colour, texture, temperature, shape...

So, excitement could be described as ...

A pulsing feeling in your chest; warm and soft; like a red pulse, causing my breathing to be high and short; a pleasant sensation which seems to spread across your chest as the excitement builds ...

What would you be THINKING (saying to yourself)?

This is all about self-talk.

It's about the tone of voice you use to yourself upon achieving this goal; the specific words you would be using. The praise you would be giving yourself.

What this process is allowing you to do is to create a complete sensory description of your Future History, it is along the lines of the process Ali used in imagining himself *celebrating a win in front of an arena full of fans days before the fight.*

To simply see the celebration without the additional sensory modes described above will not engage the mind in building a complete internal representation of the desired future.

It will not contain the emotional energy to motivate fully; nor the internal sense of completion that allows for your mind to sense the reality of your future history.

The more you put into this visualisation of your Future History the more you will align yourself to your future success. If you find any resistance to the creation of such a complete visualisation it may be that you have not fully addressed internal blocks stemming from your personal stories, values, attitudes and beliefs.

If this is the case go back to your SMARTER target and explore again the nature of your goal and the resources you need to have in place to achieve it.

Sometimes this whole process can be made easier if you are working with a coach who is well versed in this approach as they may well ask the questions you might not think of. Having said that, however, once you understand the process it is easy to use for yourself.

If you recall the SMARTER framework asked you to create a series of stepping stones in your consideration of the ACHIEVABILITY aspects of your goal.

These steps are the mini-goals which mark your progress towards your final Future History. As such they need to be spaced at meaningful intervals and have their own deadlines.

Each of these steps will therefore have a SHiFT description.

So, if my goal, dream, target was ...

Simple Statement

To enter and complete the London Marathon

Then the I would complete the SMARTER target thusly...

Measures

To have submitted an entry form

To have completed the 26 miles

Having received a time for completion

Having received medal and certificate of completion

Achievable

What is my current reality in terms of:

Fitness

Understanding of marathon rules

Understanding of training programmes

What will I need to do to create a future reality (the detail)?

1st Month : Get doctors advice on my fitness

2nd Month : Research application process

3rd Month : Research training schedules

: Find a mentor?

: Join a running club

4th Month : Start fitness training

5th Month : Run a quarter or half marathon

8th Month : Run a half marathon

9th Month : Maintain a schedule of training

9th Month : Explore diet – Carb Loading?

12th Month : Enter Marathon

Reward

I will achieve a level of fitness

I will have a sense of personal achievement

I will have raised money for a favourite charity

I will have a great story to tell

Effect

How will my training schedule have impacted on my:

family/free time

aspects of my lifestyle

desire to run more marathons

Review

At each month, as defined in the steps above (achievable) I can review my progress and adapt plans accordingly.

When I have completed this first marathon successfully I could run another; or perhaps undertake another major physical challenge; I could offer support to others who want to train; I could be a positive role model for my family and friends; I could become an advocate for a healthier lifestyle.

The specifics if each of the steps in this framework will vary, but this example gives some indication as to the required detail.

It is to this framework you will add the SHiFT descriptions.

Now here's the big tip...

**When creating a future history
build it from the FUTURE to the NOW.**

Visualise the end result, then work backwards. In this way, each step will be explored through the lens of your resources, values, attitudes and practicalities.

By way of an example...

A number of years ago I was teaching in a Secondary School in Cornwall. I was, at that time, Head of Personal and Social Education. One of my classes was a rather challenging group of Year 8 (12 -13 year olds) learners.

I decided to use the SMARTER framework and the idea of Future Histories exploring the work they would be doing in school in the context of life-long learning and achievement. I had asked all of the students to imagine that they could have any career they wanted.

This was a magic-wand exercise, so it was all about future dreams and possibilities. All of the students were happy to 'play' except one, a rather disruptive young man. He did have a bit of a reputation as being a challenging pupil, but had always been fine with me. He was also the son of a military family, so he had moved schools several times.

I sat next to him and asked him to 'play along' and to tell me that if he could be or do anything in his future, what would it be. After a little cajoling and encouragement, he offered the answer "I would love to be an astronaut". I immediately asked, 'how old do you think you would be when you are an astronaut?", he answered '34'. Which I thought was a particularly interesting answer, especially since it was such a definite one. The conversation then flowed like this ...

Me: *So, if you're an astronaut at 34, what would you have been doing at age 30?*

He: *Well I would have been in the air force as a pilot*

Me: *And at 28?*

He: *Training as a pilot*

Me: *And at 25?*

He: *Well I'd be in the RAF, training as an officer, since it's officers who become pilots*

Me: *And at 23?*

He: *Umm, guess I'd be leaving University, I think it would be easier to become an officer with a degree*

Me: *20?*

He: *At University*

Me: *18?*

He: *Finishing my "A" levels I guess...*

Me: *16?*

He:*Finishing my GCSE's*

Me:*What kind of grades would you need do you think?*

He:*Well, I guess I'd need at least a C in English, Maths and Science*

Me:*What about when you're 14?*

He:*Choosing my options....*

I made a careful note of his answers which told me one thing immediately. At some level, he had considered this career path and could talk about a meaningful progression route.

From his answers, we created a SMARTER target and a SHiFT description of each of the steps - **from the future to the now,**

Over the next few weeks his attitude to work and school appeared to change. Many of this students' teachers reported improved grades and improved behaviour. On one level, it was obvious that because someone had listened to him and taken his ideas seriously, he had allowed himself to feel more confident.

A month or so after this intervention it was parents evening, So, there I was talking to this boy's parents about his improved attitude to work and his progress. I asked them if he had shared his 'dream', they said no. I gave all of the clues about their sons 'dream' being a wish and not necessarily a reality and hoped they would understand. When this lad did finally share his 'dream' his Father immediately replied...

"An astronaut - don't be stupid son, you come from Camborne"

The lad was visibly crushed.

The next day at school he found his SMARTER plan and SHiFT descriptions and tore them up. His behaviour deteriorated and his standard of work fell.

Now, I don't think his father meant to be negative, perhaps the comment came from a place of protection - not wanting his son to be disappointed. However, as you will recognise from what you have read so far, the father was creating a story for his son; a story which without any malice possibly, limited the dreams and possibilities for his son.

Several weeks after this incident the lad came to see me, He asked if I had kept a copy of his targets. Of course, I had and he asked if he could have a copy of them. He had come to the conclusion that he 'quite liked' doing the work and that even though 'being an astronaut was a dream' he was still interested in some of the things he'd written in his plan.

At the end of Year 9 he left the school, his father had received another posting and so I never got to know how his school career panned out.

A year or so ago I received a friend request on Facebook from someone who said they were an ex-pupil of mine. I accepted the request and received a message....

"Hello, Dr Jones, do you remember me?"

I answered honestly no ...

"Well I'm the kid that wanted to be an astronaut!"

Now I remembered, so I asked how he was doing...

"Well I've just completed my degree in Astronomy and Physics and I'm about to start a Masters in Astrophysics"

I sent my congratulations and he then said...

"I'm not quite an astronaut, but I'm not far off! That plan we did, made me think about what I was really interested in and I decided if I couldn't go into space I could at least study it"

Now who is to say that this would not have been his path regardless of that conversation we had so many years ago, however it seems fair to conclude the creation of future histories supported this, now graduate, in believing in his own potential to achieve.

SHIFTING

5th Key to Exceptional Future Histories

Explore your dreams and your motivations

Create a sensory based description of your desired goal - a SHiFT Future History

Build your Future History from the FUTURE to the NOW

Use and Review SMARTER targets as you develop your Future History

Define and Own your own success - you are doing this for YOU.

Change

God grant me the serenity to accept the things I cannot change, the courage to change the things I can, and the wisdom to know the difference.

Reinhold Niebuhr

Change is the only constant in the Universe....

It was the Greek Philosopher Heraclitus of Ephesus (535 – 465 BCE) who suggested that you can't jump into the same river twice! Sounds odd I know, but in essence it's a simple statement of 'fact'. True the river may have the same name, may be in the same place as the first time you jumped in BUT the water has moved on – it's different water.

You too are different today than you were yesterday. Everything you experience, learn, think about and do changes you in some, even if very small, way. At the very least you are 24 hours older and perhaps 24 hours wiser.

Virginia Satir, the founder of conjoint family therapy, presented a model of change which suggested five clear stages, Her Change Model is quoted widely today.

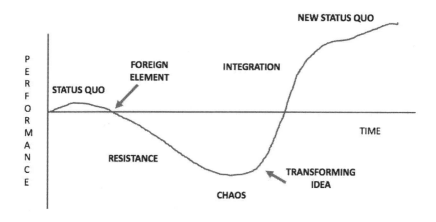

The first is the introduction of a **Foreign Element**, which could be a 'new idea', a 'new situation' or something which creates a need for change to happen.

At first, we **Resist** the idea and often try to hang on to the familiar; to the things we know; to the habits we have. This results in a sense of **Chaos**, a point we could fall back into things as they were, rather than what they could be.

If we persist on the path of change then we may reach a pivotal point – some **Transformational Idea**, allows us to see past the chaos and allows us to Integrate the new idea, behaviour, habit or situation into our lives.

Eventually we arrive at a **New Status Quo** and can look back at who, what and where we were in a more balanced way – recognising that we are doing things differently.

Within this model we can clearly see reflected Joseph Campbell's 'monomyth' as discussed in the chapter on Stories

The status quo is the prologue to our journey, the idea of change is the arrival of the message and the call to action. There is the resistance to the 'call', the desire to bury your head in the sand and ignore the challenge. Once inertia, resistance, is overcome life becomes chaotic as the journey begins. With continued motivation, you work through the chaos and eventually 'receive the elixir', the transforming idea that leads to the new status quo,

No matter what your personal history is (was) it is a part of a past that you have survived or at least brought you to where you are now. What happens next will shape your Future History. Perhaps by reviewing the following questions about past life changing moments will help you start this next one.

What was the change agent (or Foreign Element) which 'brought about' the change?

How you felt and behaved at that moment (Resistance)?

What the 'chaos' felt like for you (and how you behaved and responded)?

What was the transforming idea which led to you working with the change?

How you felt about changing your emotions, behaviours and attitudes (Integration)?

What the New Status Quo was (or is)?

Often it is the 'transforming element' that people have difficulty with. Sometimes it comes like a bolt from the blue, is totally unexpected and therefore could never be within your sphere of control.

Sometimes that transforming element is the result of a lack of decision making (action) on your own part. Sometimes you just have to 'take the bull by the horns' and do something differently.

Happiness and Freedom begin with a clear understanding of one principle. Some things are in your control and some things are not.

Epictetus

Your Future History is too important for you to wait for that lucky break or lottery win. If you are building a dream based on things outside of your control then you are giving over your future to providence, fate - you are abdicating any responsibility and thus disempowering yourself.

The thing about waiting for some 'lucky break' or 'chance event' is that it is out of your control.

True people do 'get lucky', but in terms of YOUR dreams and ambitions trusting to luck can be a very risky thing. It may take you where you want to go...

It may not....

Remember earlier the idea that change is the only constant in the Universe. Well Virginia Satir's Change Model is really a Change Cycle...

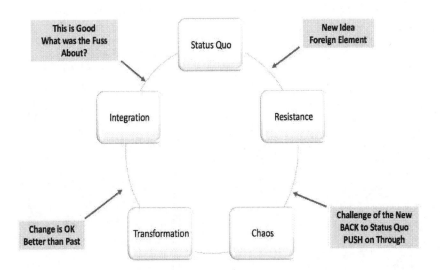

What is Personal Power?

There's a lot written about 'owning your power' or 'empowerment; but where does this power come from?

One way to consider it is that it stems from a series of internal conditions (which can be grouped under the catchall phrase - Self Esteem) and a series of external behaviours or attitudes which could be described as 'walking your talk'

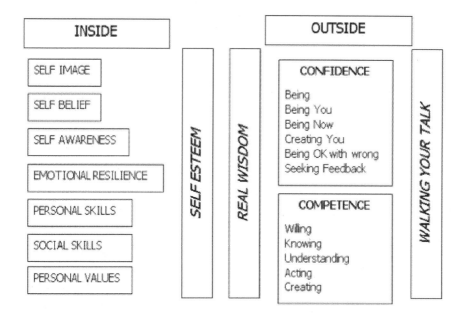

The area of 'real wisdom' alludes to the notion that it is the balance between internal and external beliefs, attitudes and behaviours which gives us our power.

If we have poor self-image or self-worth; have little or no belief in our skills and potential's we will not fully engage in our lives.

If we lack the emotional resilience to deal with set-backs, feedback or the attitudes of others we will be left at the whim and drive of other's behaviours towards us.

If we fail to develop personal and social skills then we lack the competence to act in the external world and if our value system is out of step with our self-image and/or conscious motivations then we lack conviction.

Without skills (competencies) to act, react and behave congruently in the external world we start to lack confidence and without confidence we do not take too many steps towards what could be an uncertain future.

Emotional Resilience

In simplistic terms, Emotional Resilience is the ability to adapt to stressful situations, personal crises or change (unexpected, traumatic or undesired).

Well over a decade ago, Hara Estroff Marano, Editor-at-Large for Psychology Today, wrote in an article "The Art of Resilience" in which she identified 'ten traits' of emotionally resilient individuals.

In summary, these were;

1. They know their boundaries. Resilient people understand that there is a separation between who they are at their core and the cause of their temporary suffering.

2. They keep good company. Resilient people tend to seek out and surround themselves with other resilient people, whether just for fun or when there's a need for support.

3. They cultivate self-awareness. The self-aware are good at listening to the subtle cues their body and their mood are sending.

4. They practice acceptance. Pain is painful, stress is stressful, and healing takes time. When we're in it, we want the pain to go away. When we're outside it, we want to take away the pain of those who we see suffering. Yet resilient people understand that stress/pain is a part of living that ebbs and flows.

5. They're willing to sit in silence. Being in the presence of the moment without judgment or avoidance - a practice we'd now think of as mindfulness.

6. They don't have to have all the answers. They find strength in knowing that it's okay to not have it all figured out right now and trusting that we will gradually find peace and knowing when our mind-body-soul is ready

7. They have a menu of self-care habits. They have a mental list (perhaps even a physical list) of good habits that support them when they need it most.

8. They enlist their team. The most resilient among us know how to reach out for help.

9. They consider the possibilities. We can train ourselves to ask which parts of our current story are permanent and which can possibly change. Can this situation be looked at in a different way that I haven't been considering?

10. They get out of their head. When we're in the midst of stress and overwhelm, our thoughts can swirl with dizzying speed and disconnectedness. We can find reprieve by getting the thoughts out of our head and onto our paper. As Dr. James Pennebaker wrote in his book Writing to Heal, "People who engage in expressive writing report feeling happier and less negative than before writing.

These seem to sound aspirational, attitudinal and behavioural approaches - ones we can cultivate in our own lives.

Edith Grotberg provided us with another way of thinking about the issue of resilience.

She took a I Have, I Can and I Am approach to the question. Her researches and surveys guided her to define these 15 attributes, beliefs and attitudes that served for the development of resilience

I HAVE ...

People around me I trust and who love me, no matter what

People who set limits for me ....

People who show me how to do things..

People who want me to learn to do things on my own.

People who help me ...

I AM..

A person people can like and love.

Glad to do nice things for others and show my concern.

Respectful of myself and others.

Willing to be responsible for what I do.

Sure things will be all right.

I CAN ...

Talk to others about things that frighten or bother me

Find ways to solve problems that I face.

Control myself when...

Figure out when it is a good time to talk or act...

Find someone to help me when I need it.

These can be summarised as:-

I HAVE - Love/Trust, Boundaries, Role Models, Initiative, Advocates

I AM - Self Worthy, Empathic, Respectful, Responsible, Confident

I CAN - Communicate, Think, Be aware of my Emotions, Make Decisions, Share

Those who have not had the benefit of being in and within supportive or positive relationships or have not developed any meaningful understanding of their own self and self-worth will, it could be argued, lack some degree of emotional flexibility.

Clearly restoring emotional balance; supporting the development of resilience has mental, physical, emotional and spiritual components.

All of which hints at the notion that those who are unable to develop emotional resilience may be lacking in one or more of the above 'internal', social, emotional or environmental 'attributes'. It also suggests that there is the possibility of developing those areas where there are missing elements.

This could be where SHiFT comes in again.

Imagine creating a sensory based description of the kind of you, the behaviours, of each of the ideals outlined above.

How would the I AM who can be liked and loved be described in See, Hear, Feel and Think terms?

How would the I AM who respects themselves be described in See, Hear, Feel and Think terms?

Get the idea.

What we are describing is the kind of external behaviours and internal thoughts and thoughts and feelings these attributes suggest. It's similar to what Cognitive Behavioural Therapists would ask their clients to do for situations they want to reflect upon.

Research has shown that our physiology has an effect upon our emotional state. Subjects who were told to frown whilst completing a maths test performed less well than those who were told to smile. John Grinder, one of the founders of NLP, talks about a Chain of Excellence.

Breathing effects Physiology

Physiology effects Internal State

Internal State affects Performance

And, I would add that

Performance effects Breathing

So rather than a chain, we have a cycle.

This is interesting since it means that we can start at any point in this cycle to effect changes. For some of you this may be a light-bulb moment as you will start to recognise the true value and relevance of completing a sensory based description of your goal our target.

SEEING descriptions will contain the body language information related to your Future History. As such you will have a model of the posture, expression, breathing patterns of success.

HEARING descriptions will contain auditory information that confirms and affirms the 'sound' of success.

FEELING and THINKING descriptions contain information about the 'internal state' of success.

Of course, these are hallucinations, but remember that the brain itself finds it difficult to separate reality from imagination. It is 'the self' (whatever that is) which creates qualitative distinctions between 'real' and 'imagination'; 'memory' or 'fantasy'.

What you are creating through your SHiFT descriptions are 'fully immersive' affirmations. You're not just saying the words, 'I am someone who deserves to be loved', you are breathing, standing, talking, feeling and thinking like someone who 'deserves to be loved'.

It's sad, but people make instant judgements on others based on perceptions of their 'bearing' (body language) and 'attitude' (vocal tone and intonation) within the first thirty seconds of meeting them.

Lasting impressions are formed within four minutes of any encounter. So, considering how you 'carry' yourself is important.

You will emotionally respond to others based on how you perceive them and who they remind you of from the stories of your past. This emotional response will 'leak' in your 'bearing' and 'attitude'. Being aware of this allows you to consider making the appropriate SHiFTS in how you deal with people and new situations.

CHANGE

6th Key to Exceptional Future Histories

Know that change is inevitable

Know that somethings are outside of your influence/control

Take charge of these things that are within your sphere of influence/control

Take action to meet change, do not rely on luck

Personal power can be described in terms of 'skills' that can be developed.

Personal power can also be described in terms of 'attitudes' that can be adopted

Understand that you have the power to effect changes.

Spirituality

*"The decisive question for man is: Is he related to
something infinite or not? That is the telling question of his
life. Only if we know that the thing which truly matters is the
infinite can we avoid fixing our interests upon futilities, and
upon all kinds of goals which are not of real importance.
Thus, we demand that the world grant us recognition for
qualities which we regard as personal possessions: our talent
or our beauty. The more a man lays stress on false
possessions, and the less sensitivity he has for what is
essential, the less satisfying is his life. He feels limited because
he has limited aims, and the result is envy and jealousy. If we
understand and feel that here in this life we already have a
link with the infinite, desires and attitudes change."*
Carl Jung

It is possible that, having made it this far into the book,
some of you may be wondering why I may have shied away
from discussions of spirituality. Indeed, you may have read
some of my comments about The Secret and Cosmic Ordering
have been dismissive to say the least. I don't believe that the
Universe is there to serve us, as some advocates of such
writings seem to imply. However, that does not mean that I do
not feel that we are all connected - we are One so we can
become 'in-line' with the ebb and flow of the Cosmos.

But let me back-up a moment...

We need to be clear about what we mean by spirituality. We are not talking about having a specific belief system, nor do we need to assume the existence of some Cosmic deity, benign or otherwise. Spirituality could be thought of being about having a sense of awe and wonder in the nature of existence.

In its broadest definition, spirituality is the awareness that there is something bigger than 'self'. The numerous spiritual pathways and religions which spring from this 'knowing' are ways that groups have tried to express specific pathways, with specific credos and often a specific ownership of the truth.

As we have seen during our short time together, beliefs shape perceptions and so, in a spiritual-religious sense what we accept as some form of Cosmic truth is what we find. The Universe can be seen to accommodate our labels, descriptions and limited perceptions.

In a recent training session, the conversation turned to the nature of enlightenment - what does enlightenment look, sound, feel and think like? How would we describe an enlightened person in terms of SHFT?

Perhaps we would see some of the qualities described previously?

The enlightened person could be described as being 'tranquil', 'balanced', 'reflective', 'inquisitive', 'present'?

Of course, each one of these qualities can be described in sensory-based (SHFT) terms to create even a deeper personal understanding.

So, whilst it may appear to the casual reader that we've not really been considering a spiritual journey but that of a more material path of personal motivation, we can still recognise that personal values, attitudes and codes of behaviour are (can be) spiritual.

Our personal stories, our journeys, have spiritual, physical and psychological dimensions and perhaps, to consider one in the absence of the others is a path towards personal chaos and confusion.

Our grounding is in the physical and our belief systems shape and mould our experience of the spiritual.

A Middle Path (Buddhism) or A Fourth Way (as described by Ouspensky) reminds us that this is so – indeed whilst appearances may be to the contrary, the various Mind, Body and Spirit fayres around the country today remind us of the need to bring these three facets of our experience together in a personally meaningful way.

It is a sad observation that some have minds so open that their brains fall out. Being ready to consider and reflect upon a spiritual idea is not the same as accepting blindly incoherent and incompatible philosophies which we then anguish about as they do not sit well within what we do believe, want to believe or say we believe. Such disharmony is vexatious to the spirit and sows the seeds for psychic conflict (in the Jungian sense of the word).

What we believe we perceive

Reflecting upon personal beliefs and value systems not only provides us with a spiritual starting point, but can, unless we are wary, preclude the recognition, consideration and adoption of ideas that sit outside of the experiences we define.

Remember that the human brain is a pattern matching device. It takes new experiences and tries to match them to what it knows, believes or already expects. Thus, seeing with new eyes and hearing with new ears is quite a challenge since we often have to let go of what we know (believe) in order to consider something new.

THE COSMOS

The Cosmos Seeking To Understand Itself
(Heaven)

Connection to Cosmos   Universal-Transpersonal Experience

Collective Unconscious

Spiritual Aspirations   Anima-Animus Qualities

Denied Psychic Material

Mind Senses Emotions   Sunbconscious Memories

Self-Image - Persona

Body Physical   Conscious - Ego

Who Am I?

The Individual Unwilling to Reflect Upon Themsleves
(Hell)

On the left-hand side of the diagram we see listed, in ascending order, Body, Mind and Spirit.

The Body is our physical/material frame and has such has some very specific needs.

The Mind is a generalised 'space' through which sensory information is processed and our emotions are (apparently) expressed (understood).

Our needs are met through the behaviours we engage in and our needs coupled with our emotions are fundamental drivers in terms of our motivation.

Humans can be said to have 'spiritual aspirations' through which they seek a personal connection with 'the cosmos'. These spiritual aspirations are firmly tied to our belief system, which may be limited or unlimited depending upon our knowledge, experience and wisdom.

On the right-hand side of the diagram we see listed some of the key Jungian ideas related to all that we consider to be 'us'.

Our ego is us and contrary to what some spiritual teachings suggest we do not have to shed it. It is our 'knowing' about 'us'. Ego and Egotism are two separate things.

We express these ourselves through our persona – this is our self-image. When some spiritual folk speak of letting go of ego they may actually be referring to egotism and the need for controlling the self-image(s) we are projecting.

Part of the unconscious complexes will be our 'subconscious memories'. All of that 'stuff' – the emotionally loaded associations – which can be triggered by some external event or internal thought. This is not repressed material, but simply material we are not conscious of but is nonetheless part of our experience.

Within this mix there will also be the what Jung called 'denied psychic material'. To be clear at this point Jung used the term psychic and psychic energy in the sense of 'mind' and 'mental energy' and did not imply anything about what we often call 'psychic abilities'.

This denied psychic material is stuff that was never processed by the conscious or even unconscious mind. It was put aside for later processing and may still be there until our unconscious chooses to recognise the relevance or importance of it. This material may never be brought to consciousness.

We now start to enter the 'realm' of archetypes.

The first set of 'complexes' will relate to 'animus and anima' - the notion of ideal man/woman and how we relate to each within ourselves and in our relationships.

There is then material from the 'collective unconscious' the cultural framework through which we create meaning from experience – we discussed this early.

In the diagram, I postulate three additional things.

The first is what I have called the 'universal transpersonal experience'. I sense this as the mystic state, perhaps related to the no-self idea of the Buddhists.

It is the ecstatic and possibly numinous – that is sensing the presence of divinity – state.

It could also relate to the out of the body, astral travel experiences reported by many.

I suggest in the diagram that the 'individual' unwilling to reflect upon themselves, to explore their connections with themselves, others and the cosmos may experience 'Hell'... it maybe a psychological 'hell' of unresolved complexes, uncontrolled impulses and behaviours which creates a physical 'hell'.

This is not meant to imply that atheists will fall into this 'hell' since many of the atheists I have met are very self-reflective and willing to explore their connections with each other and the Cosmos.

Carl Sagan, a well-known sceptic, scientist and atheist was able to sense the wonder of the Universe and consider our connections to it. From his writings, it is clear that he experienced 'awe' even though such a 'poetic' state was not numinous.

I would suggest that some who consider themselves to be 'spiritual' are not as self-reflective and perhaps do not achieve a 'personal balance' in terms of understanding the relationship between themselves, others and the Cosmos.

In my more provocative moments I imagine that all those conspiracy theorists, those who constantly defer to a 'them' or 'they' who are 'in control' as well as all those waiting for salvation from a rapture, or alien intelligence are living in a kind of 'hell', disempowered by the conspiracies they promote and are dependent upon Cosmic intervention before they will be 'released'.

On the other hand, I suggest in the diagram that those who are seeking to explore their connections between themselves, each other and the Cosmos actually recognise that they are 'one with the cosmos' and so find a kind of 'heaven'.

This is not a Christian heaven with angels and harps and clouds, but a knowing that they are in-tune with themselves and therefore with the Cosmos.

For me the useful thing about this 'model' is that it reminds us that all external information is processed through sensory filters, mulled over unconsciously, matched to our beliefs and other 'psychological complexes' before appearing in the consciousness as an idea, thought or inspirational message. In so many ways we make the world, the universe, the cosmos fit our accepted and expected reality rather than simply experiencing it for what it is.

Of course, this filtering, sorting and associating is vital since if our unconscious did not do this we would become overwhelmed with uncorrelated, incoherent information.

The challenge when on an academic as well as spiritual journey is to be able to side-line any preconceptions in order to make fresh assessments of what we see, hear, feel and think. The no-self state to which Buddhists aspire is not an intellectual one, but an experience of oneness with everything. In such a state, there will appear to be no boundaries between individual and the universe.

I find it interesting that in a good deal of western occultism we have all of these systems, ties and concerns about remaining connected to the physical.

Many seminal works on 'astral travel' refer to 'the silver cord' which connects the "physical body" to the "astral body" a cord which, if severed, has dire consequences for the traveller.

Time is a really interesting construct isn't it.

One of the things any meditation practitioner or ritual magician quickly realises is that our perception of time is personal and malleable. Being in an altered state removes the conscious awareness of the passage of time – it is only in the physical that we experience the flow of cause and effect.

Scientifically we know there is no reason for time not to flow in a different direction, physics can postulate effect before cause.

It seems odd then, that not only is the 'spiritual body' linked to the physical with a 'silver' or 'golden' chord but that we can also get hung up on 'past lives' and information from places and sources in the past which, in terms of an infinite universe, may not exist **yet!**

I think I'm trying to make a point here which I feel is profound and yet the words elude me.

Many, if not all, spiritual systems are created within a physical material frame of reference. They propose other dimensions and other 'non-material' places yet structure them as if they were physical.

The famous Christian Mystic Swedenborg wrote of a heaven, a life after death that consisted of real experiences in a world in many ways quite similar to the natural world. He wrote...

Angels in heaven do not have an ethereal or ephemeral existence but enjoy an active life of service to others. They sleep and wake, love, breathe, eat, talk, read, work, play, and worship. They live a genuine life in a real spiritual body and world.

Such an idea continues to be supported by numerous spiritualist mediums. Surely these are 'material' ideas and therefore 'material limitations' if taken as literal rather than metaphorical truths.

The Buddhist's view of Nirvanah seems to contain none of these 'material limitations'.

The word Nirvana means "to extinguish," such as extinguishing the flame of a candle.

This "extinguishment" is not understood by Buddhists to mean annihilation, however. Rather, it is thought of as passing into another kind of existence. In the culture in which the historical Buddha lived and taught, it was understood that fire "burns" and becomes visible when it is attached to fuel, and it stops burning and becomes invisible when it is "released" from fuel. The fire, it was thought, was not annihilated but transformed.

This 'other kind of existence' is non-describable in human terms.

Karma Mechanics

Our haste in the West to adopt Eastern religions have often over-simplified and generally confounded some key spiritual messages. Blavatsky, who was exposed to Buddhist teachings, could be said to be responsible for the over-simplification of the idea of Karma. The westernised idea of Karma and 'Karmic Law' seems to bear only the faintest trace of what Buddhism proposes.

Karma is not simply about 'lessons' and not even a kind of 'cosmic bank account' into which is stored our 'bad deeds' in order to create a spiritual overdraft which requires payment in a future life - which is how many western New Age thinkers seem to view it!

Karma is a Sanskrit word which relates to 'volitional acts'. So, as I understand it, it is about cause and effect in the sense that we need to understand that every deed is a seed which produces a fruit.

But it's not necessarily about storing up these seeds for future reward or retribution. Karma is created by the intentional acts of body, speech, and mind. Once set in motion, karma tends to continue in many directions, like ripples on a pond and to those who understand can be seen.

Now here's the thing, those 'karmic ripples' affect others.

Imagine you've had a bad day at work, you're frustrated. On the way home, you stop at the grocery store and the person at the check-out is fumbling with their change. Your frustration causes you to act impatiently and perhaps speak sharply to the person at the checkout.

Your interaction with the person at the checkout causes them upset and induces a feeling of guilt which then leads to them treating someone else with less respect.

This is Karma in action.

You could have recognised and dealt with your frustrations and so 'stopped that karma with you'.

The ripples caused by your inability to recognise, own and deal with your emotions have had broader implications. Just like butterfly wings creating a hurricane in Chaos Theory, your action could lead to some pretty major consequences for others.

Taking responsibility for your own thoughts, deeds and actions is part of the Buddhist teaching and I would argue equally important for those who pray, use affirmations and even, dare I suggest, magic for what is magic but 'karma in action'?

Being unaware of this type of cause and effect, the ripples you cast in the pond through which you swim, is being un-elightenened and so you are trapped within the ripples and locked into the wheel of the material.

Now I can almost hear a collective sigh here and the whisper – 'but isn't Karma about reincarnation?'

Well, according to Buddhist teaching ...

Any inequality between people is due not only to heredity, environment, "nature and nurture", but also to Karma. In other words, it is the result of our own past actions and our own present doings.

We ourselves are responsible for our own happiness and misery. We create our own Heaven. We create our own Hell. We are the architects of our own fate.

To clarify the concept a little more...

Karma is **action**, and Vipaka **fruit** or result, is its reaction.

Now since Buddhist doctrine is about the 'non-self' and the attainment of enlightenment by becoming 'one', what is it that reincarnates?

The simplistic notion of 'reincarnation' is one of the 'transmigration of the soul to another body after death'. Since the most fundamental doctrines of Buddhism is anatta, or anatman – there is no soul or no self, there is no permanent essence of an individual self that survives death. The simple idea of 'reincarnation' of which many speak does not seem to be part of Buddhist philosophy.

According to one Buddhist writer (Loori)

"... the Buddha's experience was that when you go beyond the skandhas, beyond the aggregates, what remains is nothing. The self is an idea, a mental construct. That is not only the Buddha's experience, but the experience of each realized Buddhist man and woman from 2,500 years ago to the present day. That being the case, what is it that dies?

There is no question that when this physical body is no longer capable of functioning, the energies within it, the atoms and molecules it is made up of, don't die with it. They take on another form, another shape.

You can call that another life, but as there is no permanent, unchanging substance, nothing passes from one moment to the next. Quite obviously, nothing permanent or unchanging can pass or transmigrate from one life to the next. Being born and dying continues unbroken but changes every moment."

Buddhism is only one view and other religions do speak of the transmigration of 'the soul'

In Jainism, the soul and matter are considered eternal, not created and perpetual.

In Hinduism's Rigveda, the oldest extant Indo-Aryan text, numerous references are made to transmigration, rebirth (punarjanma), and redeath (punarmrtyu) in the Brahmanas.

The Orphic religion, which taught reincarnation, first appeared in Thrace in north-eastern Greece and Bulgaria, about the 6th century BC, organized itself into mystery schools at Eleusis and elsewhere.

Pythagorean philosophy and reincarnation was routinely accepted throughout antiquity. In his book (Republic) Plato makes Socrates tell how Er, the son of Armenius, miraculously returned to life on the twelfth day after death and recounted the secrets of the other world.

Some early Christian Gnostic sects professed reincarnation. The Sethians and followers of Valentinus believed in it.

Of course, as an idea reincarnation is incompatible with Christian doctrine since they preach the resurrection of the faithful after death.

What is your view on Karma and in particular reincarnation?

More relevantly how does this view sit with your other belief systems?

If you believe that the spirits of the deceased can be contacted is it because they haven't reincarnated yet?

Or are spirits and souls very different things?

Is it that the spirit, personality of the deceased, hangs around whilst the soul moves on?

These are important questions, especially if you are basing your actions in this life on the challenges from a previous one or the hopes of something better later.

When I consider the idea of the *Karmic Bank* account, *be good in this life for rewards in the next,* which are held by some, I feel that at some level there is a dishonouring of the world in the here and now

Is it really a question of transcendence versus immanence?

At a recent Pagan Federation Conference Penny Billington, author and Druid, suggested that perhaps one of the reasons the Celts liked the idea of reincarnation was because the celebrated life so much they wanted more of it!

It strikes me that there are some spiritual thinkers who promote the idea that we need to quit this life and this planet at the earliest convenience.

What are they seeking an escape from?

Their own life which they feel has no value or purpose or connection?

Is such a feeling about current physical, mental or emotional illness?

Is it about a sense of isolation which will vanish once sleep, death or oblivion will cure?

Are the psychoses and neuroses about a separation of practical reality from mystical reality?

Is this life not enough?

In no way am I seeking to diminish the pain those who feel this way, rather I am wanting to believe that there are ways to balance life and spiritual stories in such a way as to bring meaning to both.

At a talk to a group of healers recently I suggested that since the word 'Healing' implied cure and cure was something no ethical complementary practitioner promised, we could perhaps use the words 'education' or 'guiding' or 'being with' as alternative descriptions. Since, for me, the idea of healing as practiced in a complementary and spiritual sense is about supporting, educating and guiding into life, through life and out of life. The way we are prepared to heal into death is as important as the way we heal into life.

What we believe about ourselves, our potential and the nature of the world in which we live actually informs us as the amount of 'power' we have to create and manage changes.

Our attitudes to change, our personal ability to accept the impermanence of any situation is a measure of how well we can answer the call to action; the invitation to the quest.

Within life and living there is death and dying – so does our personal philosophy allow for us to live with death and die with life?

Are we imagining, or even desiring, a liberation from the material world (the now); blaming some past life-effort for where and who we are (past lives) and recognition that whilst we are alive there is imperfection (transcendence versus immanence)?

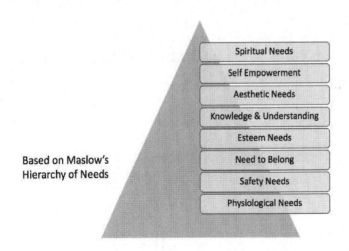

Based on Maslow's Hierarchy of Needs

Spiritual Needs

Self Empowerment

Aesthetic Needs

Knowledge & Understanding

Esteem Needs

Need to Belong

Safety Needs

Physiological Needs

In the context of some psychological thinking human needs can be seen as a hierarchy. Satisfying one leads to the drive towards the acquisition of another.

As pictured here it is a 'bit of a climb' and perhaps only available to the few who are lucky to be able to meet the needs of the previous rung of the ladder. (An idea that does not sit that comfortably with me)

Interestingly, however, you'd be hard pushed to find this kind of triangular diagram or even an allusion to it in Maslow's own work and writings.

It may be that this is the order in which we like to think things happen (similar to the where, what, who questions mentioned above), but the experience of transcendence is something I have heard reported by those who do not feel safe; who are on the fringes of 'belonging' and couldn't really care about aesthetics.

There are times I wonder if this hierarchical arrangement is part and parcel of our consumerist thinking.

First, we buy food, then safety and belonging all which implies that our needs can be met from buying and selling of experience or from being sold the idea that 'stuff' creates a 'want' which fulfils the 'need'. The so called Hedonistic Treadmill.

Experiencing the now, this moment, is about BEING and not BECOMING. Within the moment is the possibility of transcendence of the limitations of the ego self and the expansive idea that everything there is, has been or could be, is within you and around you and part of you NOW.

If we are overly worried about the 'where' of our personal or spiritual journey (as is the case within many spiritual traditions) we become overly fixated on some future state of grace and can be immobilized and made impotent in the 'here' and 'now'.

Thinking back to our questions about happiness, stories and motivations, it is worth considering our 'goal' in terms of desired states of being (or awareness or consciousness); that the challenges we face can be framed in terms of beliefs about limitations and calls for still deeper reflection.

Whatever you think you need to get 'there' is obscuring your being here

Your Life Purpose

We have been exploring the creation of personal Future Histories, and in the process of doing so have considered a number of frameworks to construct and implement them. Yet unless these future histories take into account aspects of the bigger picture of your 'journey through life' all may well be to no avail.

The search for personal authenticity, or what some may call their 'life' or 'soul' purpose contains within it some very important route-markers which may not be immediately apparent when we start upon our journey into history. They may only come to consciousness when we feel 'out of step' with who we are; when we are and where we believe we want to be.

At these moments, personal reflection is encouraged and possibly required. As Jung said ...

Your vision will become clear only when you look into your heart.

Who looks outside, dreams. Who looks inside, awakens.

He also stated....

"*There is no coming to consciousness without pain. People will do anything, no matter how absurd, in order to avoid facing their own Soul. One does not become enlightened by imagining figures of light, but by making the darkness conscious.*"

C.G. Jung

"*Thoroughly unprepared, we take the step into the afternoon of life. Worse still, we take this step with the false presupposition that our truths and our ideals will serve us as hitherto. But we cannot live the afternoon of life according to the program of life's morning, for what was great in the morning will be little at evening and what in the morning was true, at evening will have become a lie.*"

C.G. Jung

SPIRITUALITY

7th Key to Exceptional Future Histories

Explore your personal philosophies about connections

Consider conflicts between what you believe and how you act

Create personal time to reflect on the nature of nature

Reflect upon the limitations of spiritual dogma

Clearly link these ideas to your personal code of ethics

The Dream Realisation Technique

In reality, this is a set of interconnected processes based around what an individual might define as that which brings them a sense of happiness or personal fulfilment.

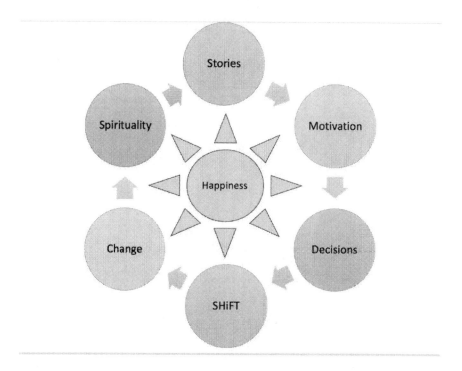

Each process and consideration is something that can stand alone, but when linked provide The Secret Keys to your Future History

About the Author

Dr Alan Jones is an NLP Trainer, Speaker, Coach and Writer.

His PhD is in Psychology and he has formal training in Hypnotherapy, Counselling, Education. Winner of two Innovation Awards for Education (Learner Motivation and Peer Mentoring), an Inspiring Human Potential Award and now Fellow of the Royal Society of Arts.

As an independent consultant and trainer, he has worked in Schools, Colleges and Universities developing coaching and impact evaluation programmes as well as learning to learn and teaching thinking initiatives. He as trained teachers at all levels up to Masters Degree.

Alan is an Accredited De Bono Thinking Skills Consultant as well as a Master Trainer in NLP.

He has worked with a range of businesses in terms of team building, management and presentation skills. He has been a tutor for the School of Social Entrepreneurs as well as for a number of other community projects.

He is co-founder of the Cornwall School of Mystery and Magick and The Fellowship of Merlin projects which allow for an exploration of the more esoteric aspects of human experience.

He has an active interest in transpersonal therapies and spirituality and, apart from being a Reiki Master, is has also worked within magical orders like B.O.T.A., Reformed Druids of Gaia and Druidic Order of the Golden Dawn. Alan is drawn to aspects of what is popularly known as Shamanism, and how cultural stories and shamanic practices are powerful tools for personal change.

In recognition of his charitable work and involvements he was made a Knight within the Ancient and Noble Order of Knights Templar (a non-denominational, non-Masonic order dedicated to charitable work) and is a member of the Fellowship of the Knights of the Round Table of King Arthur.

He is an Ambassador for the White Ribbon Campaign, men standing up to end violence towards women and girls.

Other Projects

Pagan Aid - Trustee and Volunteer Co-Ordinator

Coast FM – Community Radio Station, Broadcaster

Druid Clan of Celliwig – A Bardic inspired spiritual tradition

Working with Alan

If the ideas and approaches in this book have interested you then why not sign-up to Alan's Bootcamp courses on **Transformation TV. (www.transformation.tv)**

These courses explore in a practical way the Steps to Creating Empowering Future Histories and include further thoughts, action plans and worksheets as well as support on how to challenge yourself to achieve.

Alan has set up a closed Facebook group to discuss the issues and ideas in this book which you can find at

www.facebook.com/groups/yourfuturehistory

Websites & Social Media

www.dralanbjones.com

Facebook alanjonesUK   **Twitter** @alanjonesUK

alanjonesmindcoach   @inspirealchemy

The Research

Research that informed some of the ideas in this book.

Daily Gratitude

Volunteers were asked to make a list of five things from their day. One group were asked to reflect upon five specific events; a second group were asked to focus on five things that annoyed them and a third group to reflect upon and list five things they felt grateful for.

The Gratitude list included things like 'sunsets', 'trees', 'friends' and so.

Those compiling a gratitude list were shown to score more highly on questionnaires dealing with current levels of satisfaction and 'happiness' in their lives.

Reference

Emmons & McCullough 2003 Counting Blessings versus Burdens. An Experimental Investigation of Gratitude and Subjective well-being in daily life Journal of Personality and Social Psychology 84, 377 - 38

Talking Trauma Does Not Help

There are several pieces of research, which would be of interest to some counsellors, which suggest that talking about (hence revisiting) pain and trauma is not overly beneficial and may cause my distress than is necessary for 'healing'.

Reference

Zech & Rime; 2005 Is Talking About an Emotional Experience Helpful? Clinical Psychology & Psychotherapy 2005 12, 270 - 287

Diarising is good

The idea that keeping a personal, reflective and creative journal is familiar to many as being a useful self-development and self-therapy. Some researchers have also found that expressive writing promotes mental health and well-being.

References

Spera & Pennebaker 1994 Expressive Writing and coping with job loss

S.J. Lepore & J.M, Smyth (ads)The writing cure: How expressive writing promotes health and emotional well-being

Burton & King 2004 The Health Benefits of writing about intensely positive experiences Journal of Research in Personality 38, 150 - 163

Visualisation

Simplistic techniques of creative visualisation have been criticised by some researchers as being simple wish-fulfilment. However, when visualisation is structured, liked to goals and points of actions they seem to be of more value. In essence visualising and describing a best possible future resulted in higher scores on follow-up surveys of 'happiness' and fulfilment. In one piece of research the visualisation of best possible futures to the writing about life goals resulted in better results that simply visualising plans for day.

Reference

L A King 2001 The Health Benefits to writing about life goals

Buying Experiences

Whilst Retail Therapy in terms of buying goods may lead to retreat and self-recrimination. However the buying of experiences, doings with friends and family and just for your self, had longer lasting benefits in terms of emotional wellbeing and happiness.

Boven & Gilovich 2003 To do or to have; That is the question, Journal of Personality & Social Psychology 85, 1193 - 11202

Random Acts of Kindness

A personal sense of well-being and 'happiness' was reported as being greater amongst those who engage on random acts of kindness than those who did not.

Lyubomirsky, Sheldon & Schkade 2005 Pursuing Happiness: The Architecture of Sustainable Change Review of General Psychology 9, 111 - 131

Physiology and Performance

In mathematic test where individuals wee asked to either slouch or sit-up straight. Those who sat-up performed better than those who did not.

Reference

Roberts & Arefi-Afsha Not all who stand tall are proud: Gender differences in the proprioceptive effects of upright posture Cognition& Emotion 21, 714-17

In a similar trial smiling or frowning influenced how people evaluated projects and products. Those who smiled gave higher (more positive) evaluations.

Reference

Forster 2004 How body feedback influences Consumers evaluation of products Journal of Consumer Psychology 14, 415 – 425

Happiness Rules!

Researchers across several fields have suggested that attaining what could be defined as 'happiness' encourages personal achievement across several 'life' domains including relationships, marriage, work performance, income and health. It appears that these things were not the things that brought happiness rather that attaining 'happiness' (possibly with all of the things we described in the chapter on Happiness) led to them; they were the by product of happiness.

Reference

Lyubomirsky, S., King, L., & Diener, E. (2005). The Benefits of Frequent Positive Affect: Does Happiness Lead to Success? Psychological Bulletin, 131(6), 803-855.

Money does not bring Happiness

If personal goals are driven by the acquisition of money then research has found that people often underestimate the effects it will have on other life goals. More time is allocated or leaks towards acquiring things rather than enjoying life. Hence 'happiness' could be seen as inversely proportional to wealth. So much depends upon what is done with what is acquired and how personal time is balanced.

Reference

Richard A. Easterlin, 2003 11176–11183 Proceedings of the National Academy of Sciences of North America

Owning you own Goals

There seems to be a clear link between motivation and identifying what is within the scope of an individuals 'control'. More relevantly goals that are created within a framework of self-efficacy are more likely to be achieved

Reference

Phillips, Jean M., Gully, Stanley M. 1997   Journal of Applied Psychology, Vol 82(5), Oct 1997, 792-802

Endnotes

"Surround Yourself with Positive People Who Believe in Your Dreams

Distance yourself from negative people who try to lower your motivation and decrease your ambition. Create space for positive people to come into your life.

Surround yourself with positive people who believe in your dreams, encourage your ideas, support your ambitions, and bring out the best in you."

Roy T Bennett

Made in the USA
Columbia, SC
21 June 2018